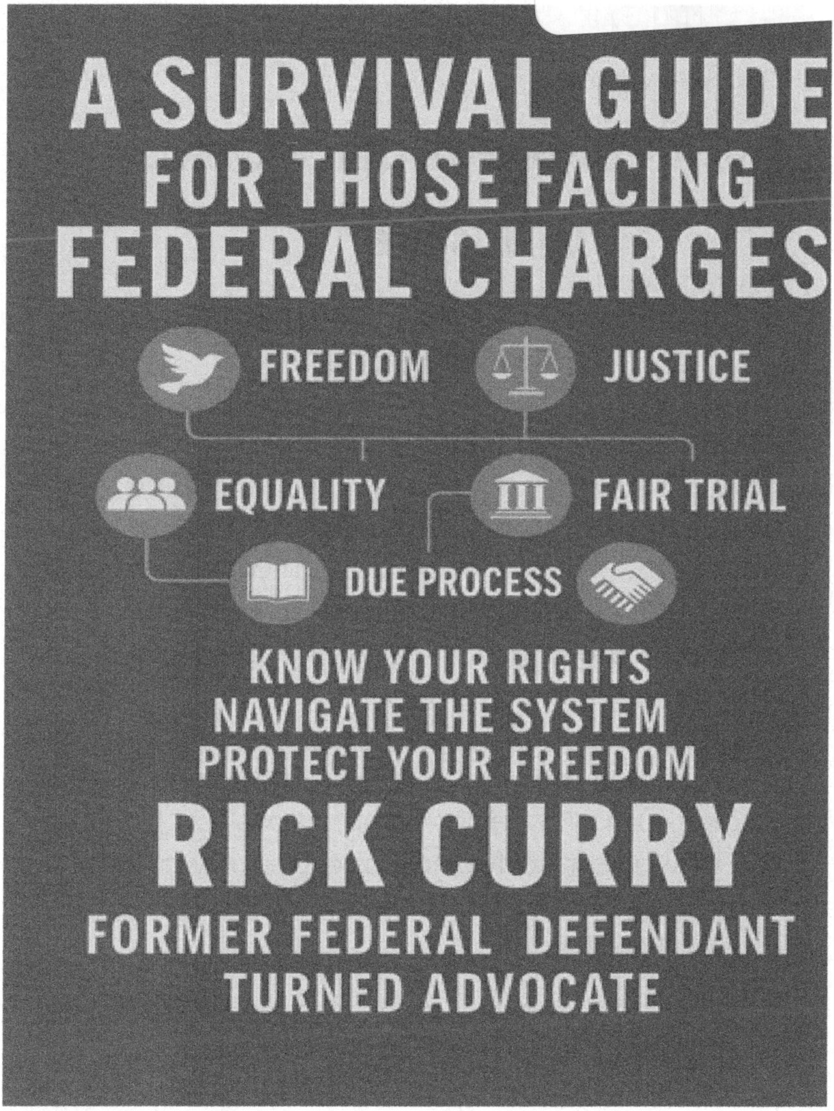
A SURVIVAL GUIDE
FOR THOSE FACING
FEDERAL CHARGES
FREEDOM
JUSTICE
EQUALITY
FAIR TRIAL
DUE PROCESS
KNOW YOUR RIGHTS
NAVIGATE THE SYSTEM
PROTECT YOUR FREEDOM
RICK CURRY
FORMER FEDERAL DEFENDANT
TURNED ADVOCATE

The Accused Federal Guide To Justice

SURVIVAL GUIDE FOR THOSE FACING FEDERAL CHARGES

This handbook is organized to change the way most criminal defendants approach criminal court proceedings based on an allegation of an offense that has been committed by the accused. It explains in detail the planning process to challenge legal rulings and vindicate the accused. Moreover, it teaches the accused the defense method(s) by recommending ways to carefully plan legal applications to challenge the unwarranted federal charges. Always consult with a legal attorney when faced with a federal criminal matter.

The law affects the lives of all American citizens and other foreign inhabitants in its legal jurisdiction whether you are a foreign-born resident or not. The federal laws regulate lawful and unlawful activities and have consequences. We may or may not be conscious of them but, if there comes a time when we need to be aware of the law's presence, this handbook is simplified to help you understand the law, its unfamiliar terms, and possible criminal defense techniques in detail for easier comprehension.

Many entries in this book include United States Supreme court case laws, appellate court case laws, and federal statutes. The legal terminology explains specific legal applications when dealing with the law under the United States federal criminal system. The information provided in this handbook is presented in a style that will be familiar to all users that have been exposed to federal criminal prosecution. The publisher and author take no responsibility for any of the methods described in this book but would like to assure you that the methods are common and correct when appropriately applied.

The Accused Federal Guide to Justice: A Survival Guide for Those Facing Federal Charges by the Feds, DEA, or ATF is the real talk manual for anyone facing federal charges. No fluff, no legalese—just strategies, breakdowns, and the truth about how to survive and fight smart in the federal system.

Publisher: Rick Curry

Title of Book: *The Accused Federal Guide to Justice Handbook: A Survival Guide for Those Facing Federal Charges by the Feds, DEA, or ATF*

This book aims to provide practical advice and guidance to the individual who finds him/herself navigating the complexities of the federal justice system.

I am an ex federal offender that served more than 25 years in the system. Through my experience and expertise, I have learned and encountered firsthand the challenges and uncertainties that accompany being accused in a federal legal system. Throughout my experience and research, I have developed a comprehensive understanding of the legal process and the emotional and practical implications it carries for the accused.

1. Understanding the federal legal system, an overview of the federal justice system including key terminology, legal processes, and institutions

2. Navigating legal proceedings, practical guidance on court appearances, legal representation and understanding legal documentation

3. Emotional and logical support strategies for coping with the emotional toll of being accused and maintaining mental well-being throughout the legal process

4. Building a support network, and advice on seeking and utilizing support from family, friends, and relevant organizations

5. Moving forward, exploring life after the legal process includes rebuilding one's reputation and pursuing personal and professional goals

Table of Contents

Introduction To the Federal Legal System

The federal legal system in the United States operates under a framework that balances the powers between the national government and the individual states. The federal legal system is designed to interpret and apply the laws passed by Congress, the Executive branch, and the Courts. Here's an overview of its operations:

Structure of the Federal Legal System

- **Federal Constitution**: The foundation of the U.S. legal system is the U.S. Constitution, which sets out the structure of the federal government, the powers of its three branches, and the rights of citizens.
- **Congress**: The legislative branch of the federal government, consisting of the Senate and the House of Representatives, makes laws that apply at the federal level.
- **Executive Branch**: Led by the President, the executive branch enforces federal laws, including regulatory agencies.
- **Judicial Branch**: The judicial branch interprets and applies federal laws and is led by the U.S. Supreme Court, with lower courts (Court of Appeals and District Courts) handling cases at different levels.

Jurisdiction of Federal Courts: Federal courts have jurisdiction over cases that involve federal law, interstate disputes, issues between states, and cases involving the federal government. Federal courts also hear cases in which citizens of different states are involved, as well as cases dealing with treaties, the Constitution, and cases where the U.S. is a party.

The Role of the U.S. Supreme Court: The U.S. Supreme Court is the highest court in the country and serves as the final authority on interpreting the Constitution and federal law. The Court has appellate jurisdiction, meaning it primarily reviews decisions made by lower federal and state courts.

Federal Laws: Federal laws are enacted by Congress and applied uniformly across the country. These laws deal with matters such as civil rights, immigration, taxation, intellectual property, and national security. Federal regulations and executive orders further define and implement these laws.

Checks and Balances: The federal system operates under the principle of checks and balances, where each branch of government can limit the powers of the other branches. For example, while Congress can pass laws, the President has the power to veto them, and the judiciary can rule laws unconstitutional.

Cases in the Federal Legal System: Cases in the federal system are typically those that involve federal statutes, constitutional issues, or disputes between parties from different states. These cases begin in federal district courts, which are organized by geographical regions. Appeals from these courts go to the U.S. Courts of Appeals, and, if necessary, cases can be escalated to the U.S. Supreme Court.

This structure ensures that laws are applied consistently across the United States, protecting citizens' rights and maintaining justice within the framework of federal governance.

As an accused and a convicted ex-felon, I believe The Accused Federal Guide to Justice has the potential to provide valuable support and empowerment to the individuals facing federal legal challenges. This book is written in a clear and accessible style, combining personal insight, practical advice, and resources for the accused.

The term accused typically refers to an individual who has been formally charged with or accused of committing a crime or an offense. This could occur in a legal context such as when a person is brought before a court of law and is formally accused of wrongdoings by the prosecuting authority.

The accused is the individual who is alleged to have committed the offense and is entitled to certain legal rights and protections including the perception of innocent until proven guilty.

The federal legal system in many countries including United States operate based on a framework of laws, courts and enforcement agencies that are responsible for upholding and interpreting the laws. The information in this book will only relate to the federal laws on the level that is simplified for an overview of how the federal legal system typically runs.

General Information You Should Know

United States – Federal Indictments & Incarceration rates

1. How many people are federally indicted each year?

- Federal indictments typically range from **70,000 to 90,000 per year**, depending on the year.
- These indictments are handled by **U.S. Attorneys' Offices**, and cover federal crimes (drug trafficking, fraud, immigration violations, etc.).

2. How many people are incarcerated each year in the U.S.?

- There are two types of incarceration: federal and state/local.
- Total incarcerated population (2023 estimate):
  About **1.9 to 2 million people** are incarcerated at any given time in the U.S.
    - Federal prisons: ~145,000 inmates
    - State prisons: ~1 million
    - Local jails: ~750,000
- Each year, millions of people cycle through the system (especially jails, due to short-

term detentions). Around 600,000–700,000 people are released from prisons annually.

- The United States is the country with the highest incarceration rate. Measured over the past 3 recent years as inmates per 100,000 people, the U.S. has consistently had the highest incarceration rate:

Year	Incarceration Rate (per 100,000)
2021	~639
2022	~625
2023	~621

- The next highest countries (usually far behind) are Rwanda (~500 per 100,000), Seychelles (~480–500), and El Salvador, which increased dramatically in 2022–2023, potentially over 600 per 100,000 due to a crackdown on gangs. So, while El Salvador may have temporarily surpassed the U.S. recently due to emergency policies, the **U.S. has had the highest incarceration rate for decades**.

3. How many people are in federal custody in the United States?

- Total: ~195,000 people

- As of the most recent data (late 2023–early 2024), here's a breakdown of the number of people in federal custody. This includes federal prisons, jails, halfway houses, and other forms of custody:

Category	**Approximate Count**
Federal Bureau of Prisons (BOP) – incarcerated in federal prisons	~145,000
Privately managed contract facilities (immigration-related, etc.)	~14,000
Residential Reentry Centers (halfway houses + home confinement)	~10,000–12,000
Pretrial detainees in U.S. Marshals Service custody	~30,000
Others (e.g., military, D.C. Code offenders, etc.)	~2,000–3,000

Note: Numbers fluctuate due to policies, prosecutions, and releases. To find information on the number of individuals indicted federally each year, you can use the Federal Criminal Case Processing Statistics (FCCPS) Tool provided by the

Bureau of Justice Statistics. This interactive tool allows you to query data on federal criminal case processing, including indictments, prosecutions, and sentencing.

Definitions

BOP custody: Long-term federal inmates serving sentences.

Residential Reentry Centers (RRCs): Transitional housing for inmates near the end of their sentence or on supervised release.

U.S. Marshals Custody: Pretrial detainees awaiting trial or sentencing, often held in local jails under federal contract.

Overview of key federal laws and legislative frameworks that govern how people end up in federal custody, what laws apply, and how incarceration is managed:

I. Laws and Legislation: Federal Level (U.S.)

1. U.S. Constitution

- **Fifth Amendment**: Due process protections
- **Eighth Amendment**: Prohibits cruel and unusual punishment
- These set the foundation for all laws governing detention and incarceration.

2. Major Federal Criminal Laws (Statutes)

a. Title 18 – U.S. Code (Crimes and Criminal Procedure)

- The **primary body of federal criminal law**.
- Covers crimes like:
  - Drug trafficking (e.g., 21 U.S.C. § 841)
  - Fraud, bribery, and white-collar crimes
  - Immigration offenses
  - Firearms offenses
  - Terrorism-related crimes

b. Title 21 – U.S. Code (Controlled Substances Act)

- Governs **drug-related federal offenses**
- Mandatory minimum sentences still apply in many drugs cases

3. Sentencing Guidelines

- **U.S. Sentencing Guidelines (USSG)** – issued by the U.S. Sentencing Commission
- Judges use them to determine sentence lengths
- They are *advisory*, not mandatory (since *U.S. v. Booker*, 2005)

4. Federal Bureau of Prisons (BOP) Authority

Governed by **Title 18, Chapter 303–313**

- BOP manages all aspects of **custody, rehabilitation, classification, transfer, and release** of federal inmates.

5. Key Legislation Impacting Incarceration & Release

Law	Year	What It Did
Sentencing Reform Act	1984	Established the Sentencing Commission; eliminated parole in federal cases
Violent Crime Control & Law Enforcement Act	1994	Expanded prison funding, added mandatory sentences
Prison Litigation Reform Act (PLRA)	1996	Restricted inmates' ability to sue over prison conditions
First Step Act	2018	Major reform; reduced some mandatory minimums, expanded good-time rehabilitation programs

6. Custody Types Under Federal Law

- **Pretrial Detention**: Based on risk of flight or danger (Bail Reform Act of 1984)
- **Post-Conviction Custody**: BOP oversees imprisonment.
- **Home Confinement / Halfway Houses**: Expanded under First Step Act
- **Supervised Release**: Replaces parole in federal system.

7. Current Legislative Focus (2023–2025)

Congress and advocates are considering:

- Expanding **compassionate release**
- Addressing **overincarceration** and racial disparities
- Reforming **mandatory minimums**
- Improving **prison conditions**, especially in private prisons
- Increased use of **alternatives to incarceration** (diversion, mental health courts). You can find key legislation impacting incarceration and release at the following site: http://www.congress.gov.

Information Concerning Federal Indictments & Complaints

In federal criminal cases, an accused defendant does not always have to be arrested on an indictment. A defendant can be arrested on a criminal complaint before an indictment is handed down. Here's how that process works and how state and federal law enforcement interact in these cases:

1. Arrest on a Complaint vs. Indictment:

- Criminal Complaint: A criminal complaint is a written statement of the charges against a defendant, typically filed by a law enforcement officer. It is used in the early stages of a federal case, often leading to an arrest before the formal indictment. A complaint can be filed by law enforcement and presented to a magistrate judge, who then issues an arrest warrant if a probable cause is established. The complaint provides enough probable cause to arrest the defendant and bring them before the court, but it does not yet represent a formal charge like an indictment.
- Indictment: An indictment is a formal charge issued by a grand jury, which occurs later in the legal process after the initial arrest. This is the formal, written

accusation of a crime and is required in felony cases for federal charges under the Fifth Amendment (except in cases where a defendant waives their right to a grand jury). If the grand jury finds sufficient evidence, they issue an indictment.

In summary, an arrest can be made based on a criminal complaint, which can then lead to an indictment.

2. Federal Agencies Involved in Investigations:

Various federal agencies are involved in conducting investigations depending on the nature of the crime. These agencies include, but are not limited to:

- Federal Bureau of Investigation (FBI): Handles a wide range of criminal investigations, including terrorism, cybercrime, organized crime, and public corruption.
- Drug Enforcement Administration (DEA): Focuses on drug-related crimes, including trafficking and distribution.
- Bureau of Alcohol, Tobacco, Firearms, and Explosives (ATF): Investigates firearms violations, explosives, arson, and alcohol/tobacco trafficking.
- U.S. Secret Service: Protects federal officials and investigates financial crimes like

counterfeiting, credit card fraud, and identity theft.

- U.S. Marshals Service: Responsible for apprehending fugitives, managing prisoner transport, and witness protection.
- Customs and Border Protection (CBP) and Immigration and Customs Enforcement (ICE): Investigate crimes related to immigration, human trafficking, and customs violations.

3. Role of State Law Enforcement in Federal Investigations:

State law enforcement agencies often collaborate with federal agencies during investigations, especially when the crime crosses state lines or involves federal jurisdiction (e.g., drug trafficking, interstate crime, terrorism). These state agencies may provide assistance in terms of manpower, local knowledge, and access to state-level resources.

- For example, local police might assist in tracking down suspects, executing warrants, or providing information relevant to an investigation that federal agencies are handling.
- In some cases, state law enforcement may initiate investigations and work with federal

agencies to pursue federal charges once the case escalates to that level.

4. Can a Federal Indictment Proceed Without Federal Agencies' Involvement?

Generally, federal indictments require the involvement of federal agencies, as they typically investigate federal crimes. However, in certain circumstances:

- State Investigations Leading to Federal Charges: A state or local law enforcement agency can conduct an investigation into a crime that has a federal nexus (e.g., a crime involving interstate commerce, federal statutes, or federal property). If the investigation uncovers enough evidence to justify federal charges, federal prosecutors (U.S. Attorneys) may take over the case and seek an indictment.
- Parallel State and Federal Investigations: It's also possible for both federal and state agencies to work on an investigation concurrently. A state agency may handle certain aspects of a case, while federal agencies pursue other aspects, and federal prosecutors ultimately bring the case before a grand jury for an indictment.

In short, while state law enforcement can initiate certain investigations, especially in cases that may have federal implications, a federal indictment typically involves the work of federal agencies due to the nature of federal jurisdiction. The role of state law enforcement will depend on the nature of the case and the level of cooperation between federal and state authorities.

Waiving the Right to an Indictment

When an accused federal defendant is arrested based on a complaint and arraigned before a judge, the judge might offer the defendant the opportunity to waive their right to an indictment by a grand jury. This right is protected under the Fifth Amendment to the U.S. Constitution, which guarantees that felony charges be brought by an indictment by a grand jury. However, the defendant can choose to waive this right and proceed with information (a formal charging document filed by a prosecutor without grand jury involvement).

Reasons to Waive the Right to Indictment (Good Reasons)

1. Faster Process:

    - Speedy Resolution: Waiving the grand jury indictment can speed up the process. If the defendant is eager to resolve their case quickly, they might waive the indictment, especially if they want to move towards plea negotiations or trial sooner.

- Avoiding a Long Wait: The grand jury process can sometimes take weeks or months, depending on the complexity of the case, so waiving it allows for a more immediate focus on pretrial motions, discovery, and trial preparation.

2. Plea Bargaining Considerations:

    - Potential Plea Deals: Some defendants may believe that waiving the indictment and agreeing to an information will lead to a more favorable plea deal, as it can be seen as a gesture of cooperation or a way to move past the grand jury phase and get to negotiations more quickly.

3. Legal Strategy:

    - Reduction in Complexity: In some cases, waiving the indictment could reduce the complexity of the case. Grand jury proceedings are generally secret, and waiving indictment might give both sides clearer insight into the charges and evidence, which could lead to better-informed decisions.

Reasons to NOT Waive the Right to Indictment (Bad Reasons)

1. Lack of Full Discovery:
    - Not Enough Information: If the defendant waives the right to an indictment too quickly, they might not have a full understanding of the case against them. The grand jury proceedings involve witnesses and evidence that could reveal crucial information. By waiving this right, the defendant could miss out on valuable insight into the government's case.
2. Potential for Grand Jury Exoneration:
    - Opportunity for Grand Jury Review: A grand jury serves as a safeguard against unjust prosecutions, providing an impartial body to review whether there's enough evidence to proceed. If the defendant waives the indictment, they lose this safeguard, which could prevent the indictment from moving forward if the grand jury decides there's insufficient evidence.
3. Preserving Rights and Legal Processes:
    - Ensuring Due Process: The grand jury process ensures that the defendant's rights are properly safeguarded. If a defendant waives this right, they may feel pressured or

rushed into decisions without fully considering the potential consequences.

4. Possible Legal Errors:

   - Waiving Under Pressure: Defendants might waive the indictment without fully understanding the legal implications, especially if they're under pressure from their attorney, the prosecution, or due to personal circumstances (e.g., fear of prolonged legal proceedings or jail time). This could lead to a loss of important legal rights.

Expiration of the Complaint and Timely Indictment

In federal criminal cases, a complaint is typically only valid for a limited period, often **30 days**. This means that after the complaint is filed and an arrest is made, the government must present evidence to a grand jury and secure an indictment within that time frame, or the case could be dismissed. This timeline is critical for the following reasons.

What Happens if an Indictment Is Not Timely Filed?

1. Dismissal of Charges:

   If the government fails to bring an indictment in a timely manner, the case could be dismissed due to lack of timely prosecution. The expiration of the complaint without a formal indictment means the government has not followed the necessary legal procedures, and the charges may no longer be valid.

2. Defendant's Right to Speedy Trial:

   The Sixth Amendment guarantees a defendant the right to a speedy trial. If the government delays too long in securing an indictment or fails to follow up on a complaint within the statutory period, this could potentially violate the defendant's right to a speedy trial, and the case may be dismissed on these grounds.

3. Legal Protections for the Defendant:

   The timely filing of an indictment ensures that the defendant's rights are upheld, particularly the right to know the specific charges against them. If an indictment is not filed and the complaint expires, the defendant could argue that they were not adequately informed of the charges in time, and the case might be dismissed as a result.

4. Government's Burden:

   Failure to secure an indictment within the time frame is typically seen as a failure by the government to meet its burden of proof in the case. While this could potentially allow for dismissal, it can also be an opportunity for the government to present stronger or clearer evidence if they choose to refile charges.

Possible Consequences of Expiration

- Refiling the Case: If the complaint expires without an indictment, the prosecution can refile the charges, but they may need to present new evidence or go through the entire process again.
- Dismissal on Procedural Grounds: Depending on the circumstances and the judge's discretion, the defendant seeks a dismissal of the case for failure to proceed in a timely manner.

In Summary:

- Waiving the right to an indictment might offer the defendant a faster process, but it also means forfeiting the grand jury's review of the case, which could have revealed weaknesses in the government's evidence.
- If the complaint expires and no indictment is filed on time, the case could be dismissed, and the defendant may be free from prosecution unless the charges are refiled within the allowed time frame. The expiration of the complaint and failure to indict in a timely manner is a critical procedural safeguard for the defendant, ensuring their right to a fair trial and protection from unnecessary delays.

Another reason why it would not be a good idea to plead guilty to a complaint is because you may not get indicted within 30 days, which is the allowable time for the prosecutor to pursue the grand jury on the charges once the complaint is filed in federal court. If the charges are not brought up under an indictment within 30 days, then the accused has to be released automatically, and those same charges can't be pursued in a new filing of the indictment in a case against the accused based on double jeopardy, meaning the government would have to find some other charges to indict you on.

Accused Indictment Should Be Set Up Like This

1. Caption (Heading)

- **Names of the parties**: The plaintiff and the defendant(s) are listed here.
  - **Court Information**: The name of the court where the case is being filed.
    - **Case Number**: This is assigned by the court when the case is filed.
      - **Title of the Case**: Typically, "Plaintiff v. Defendant."

2. Jurisdiction and Venue

- **Jurisdiction** refers to the court's authority to hear the case, and in the case of a federal complaint, it is often based on federal laws, diversity of citizenship, or other federal statutes.
- **Venue** specifies the proper location for the case to be heard within the federal court system.

3. Parties

- This section identifies the plaintiff(s) and defendant(s), including their names and addresses. It may also identify whether any defendant is a government agency or an entity like a corporation.

4. Statement of Claims (or Causes of Action)

- This is the main body of the complaint. It outlines the specific legal claims the plaintiff is making against the defendant(s).
- The plaintiff will describe the alleged wrongdoing (e.g., breach of contract, discrimination, negligence, etc.) and cite the relevant legal principles(constitutional rights, statutory law, or common law principles) that support the claims.
- Each claim should be numbered and clearly stated.

5. Factual Allegations

- This section provides a detailed narrative of the facts that support the plaintiff's claims. It answers the "what happened" question, including relevant dates, events, and actions that led to the dispute.
- The facts must be presented in a way that justifies the legal claims being made.

6. Request for Relief (Prayer for Relief)

- In this part, the plaintiff specifies what they want from the court. This could include:
  - **Compensatory damages** (money to compensate for harm),
    - **Punitive damages** (money meant to punish the defendant),
      - **Injunctive relief** (orders to do or stop doing something),
        - **Declaratory relief** (a declaration of the parties' rights),

- Other remedies are specific to the case.

7. Signature and Verification

- The complaint must be signed by the attorney or the plaintiff if representing themselves.
- In some cases, the complaint may need to be verified (sworn to be true) before being filed with the court.

8. Exhibits (Optional)

- Documents, photographs, contracts, or other evidence that support the plaintiff's claims may be attached as exhibits to the complaint.

Key Points:

- **Federal jurisdiction**: A federal complaint must demonstrate that the federal court has jurisdiction over the case. This can be based on a federal question (e.g., violation of federal law or the Constitution) or diversity jurisdiction (where the parties are from different states and the amount in controversy exceeds $75,000).

- **Filing and Service**: Once the complaint is filed with the court, it must be served on the defendant(s), meaning the defendant(s) must be officially notified about the lawsuit. Service of process is a required step before the defendant can respond.

- A federal complaint is the starting point in a federal lawsuit, and the defendant will typically respond with an answer, motion to dismiss, or other legal response. It's essential that the complaint is carefully drafted to meet legal standards and effectively present the case.

Key Differences Between a Criminal Federal Complaint & Indictment:

Feature	**Criminal Federal Complaint**	**Indictment**
Initiation	Filed by law enforcement or prosecutor	Issued by a grand jury
Who Reviews the Evidence	Judge (for probable cause)	Grand jury (citizens)
Type of Charges	Misdemeanors or felonies	Generally, felonies
Process	Filed by a prosecutor or officer with an affidavit	Formal charge after grand jury proceedings
Purpose	To charge a defendant	To formally accuse

Feature	Criminal Federal Complaint	Indictment
	quickly and establish probable cause for arrest	someone of a felony and start the process for trial
Legal Requirement	Often used in the early stages of a case, especially for misdemeanors	Required for felony charges in the federal system

Federal Criminal Complaint and Statute of Limitations:

A federal criminal complaint is used to initiate criminal charges, typically in the early stages of a case. The statute of limitations for a criminal complaint is the same as the statute of limitations for the underlying crime it is based on.

- The statute of limitations is the period of time after a crime occurs within which charges must be filed. If charges are not filed within this time frame, the defendant can no longer be prosecuted for that crime.
- **For federal crimes**, the statute of limitations can vary widely depending on the nature of

the offense. Some crimes have very short time limits, while others have longer periods. For example:

- **Most federal felonies**: Typically have a **5-year statute of limitations** (e.g., fraud, drug offenses).
- **Some federal crimes** (e.g., certain terrorism-related offenses or child exploitation): May have a **10-year statute of limitations**.
- **Other serious offenses**: Certain crimes, such as **murder**, **war crimes**, and **terrorism**, may have **no statute of limitations** at all, meaning charges can be filed at any time.

- The **clock** for the statute of limitations generally begins from the date crime is committed. However, in some cases, the clock may be extended if:
  - The defendant is **fleeing** from justice or avoiding detection.
  - The **victim** of a crime has not yet discovered the crime (as fraud cases).

Federal Indictment and Statute of Limitations:

A federal indictment is a formal charge issued by a grand jury, and it is used to bring a defendant to trial for a felony charge. The statute of limitations for a federal indictment depends on the nature of the crime being charged, just like with a criminal complaint:

- **Most federal crimes**: The statute of limitations is typically **5 years.**

- **Fraud-related crimes** (e.g., wire fraud, bank fraud, or identity theft): Generally, have a **5-year statute of limitations.**

- **Sexual assault of minors** or **child pornography**: Some of these crimes may have extended periods, sometimes up to **10 years** or more, depending on the circumstances.

- **Terrorism or war crimes**: These crimes often have **no statute of limitations**, meaning the government can bring charges at any time.

- **Murder**: There is **no statute of limitations** for murder under federal law.

Key Points to Keep in Mind:

- **The statute of limitations applies to the crime itself**, not just the document (whether it's a complaint or an indictment). The government must charge the defendant before the statute of limitations expires.

- **Tolling**: In some circumstances, the statute of limitations can be "tolled" (paused or extended), such as when the defendant is outside the United States or concealing their identity.

- **Federal crimes with no statute of limitations**: As mentioned, serious crimes like terrorism, war crimes, and murder can be prosecuted at any time, no matter how many years have passed.

In Summary:

- Both federal criminal complaints and federal indictments are subject to statutes of limitations, which vary depending on the crime.

- Most federal crimes have a 5-year statute of limitations, but certain offenses like murder and terrorism have no time limit at all.

Adequate Representation

The United States constitution provide the accused with legal aid: the right to an attorney, in the United States constitution primarily addressed in the Sixth Amendment to the United States constitution the ruling part of the Sixth Amendment states" in all criminal prosecutions the accused shall enjoy the right to have the assistance of counsel for his defense". This provision guarantees individuals the right to have an attorney to represent them in criminal cases.

It has been interpreted to mean that the government must provide an attorney for those who cannot afford one. Additionally, the Supreme Court case Gideon versus Wainwright (1963), clarified that the right to council applies to state criminal proceedings through the Fourteenth Amendment due process clause as a result of this decision all individuals facing the possibility of imprisonment have the right to be provided with an attorney if they cannot afford one. The Sixth Amendment right to counsel is a fundamental protection in the United States legal system to ensure that individuals have legal representation when facing criminal charges.

See: The **U.S. Constitution** provides the right to legal representation for criminal defendants through the **Sixth Amendment**. Specifically, the Sixth Amendment guarantees that "In all criminal prosecutions, the accused shall enjoy the right…to have the Assistance of Counsel for his defense."

This right to counsel is meant to ensure that criminal defendants, regardless of their ability to pay for an attorney, are provided with legal representation. This principle has been expanded through various court decisions, including the landmark case of **Gideon v. Wainwright (1963)**. The U.S. Supreme Court ruled in Gideon that the right to counsel is fundamental to a fair trial and applies to state criminal defendants as well as federal ones, meaning that indigent defendants (those who cannot afford an attorney) must be provided one at the government's expense.

Federal Criminal Justice Act (CJA) for Indigent Defendants

The **Federal Criminal Justice Act (CJA)** is a law that provides the structure for appointing counsel to indigent defendants in federal criminal cases. The key features of the CJA include:

1. **Eligibility**: Indigent defendants (those who cannot afford to hire an attorney) in federal criminal cases are entitled to have counsel appointed at the expense of the government. If a defendant demonstrates they lack the financial means to afford an attorney, the court will appoint one for them.

2. **CJA Panel Attorneys**: In federal cases, there are CJA Panel Attorneys who are experienced criminal defense lawyers who are appointed by the court to represent indigent defendants. These attorneys are typically compensated at an hourly rate set by the judiciary, though the amount may not reflect the full value of their work.

3. **Payment**: The CJA provides compensation for defense attorneys in federal cases. The rates for attorney compensation and expert fees are capped by federal guidelines, but the government reimburses lawyers for their services and may also cover certain investigative or expert costs. In cases where the appointed attorney's services go beyond the standard, they may request additional funds for necessary expenditures.

4. **CJA Fund**: The CJA Fund is the financial resource used by the courts to pay for the costs of appointed defense counsel, as well as other necessary costs such as investigative services and expert witnesses, in federal criminal cases. It ensures that indigent defendants can access these critical services without having to pay out-of-pocket.

5. **Pro Bono Representation**: In some cases, lawyers may represent indigent client's pro bono (without payment) if they are willing to do so, although the CJA exists to cover those costs when no volunteer attorney is available.

In summary, the **Sixth Amendment** guarantees a criminal defendant's right to counsel, and the **Federal Criminal Justice Act (CJA)** ensures that indigent defendants in federal cases have access to legal representation, with the government providing funding for their defense counsel and other related services.

The term **Due Process** at a minimum means that a citizen who will be affected by a government decision must be given advanced notice of what the government plans to do and how the government's actions may deprive them of life liberty or property. Basically, the due process states that you shall have your day in court before they can take any of that away from you as the accused, life, liberty or property.

Bond & Detained Information

Whether the accused enters a plea of not guilty or guilty at their arraignment, most likely in all cases they will be issued a bond hearing. Not saying they will be awarded or granted a bond through the court's proceedings, which will be determined based on flight risk and other information . The Judge would evaluate to see if the accused poses a harm to the general public **or anyone specifically that the judge could use to either deny the** bond or give a bond that's reasonable. One that could be met by the accused.

If the accused can make the bond, it is a good thing to be out on bond while preparing a defense or strategy for the government's case against them.

If the accused individual is not fortunate enough to obtain a bond and must be incarcerated until they either plead guilty and enter a plea deal or go to trial. They should not share information about their case with people who are incarcerated with them. A lot of times these individuals find ways to appear in the prosecution process of the accused by offering information that they say was expressed to them by the accused to the prosecuting authorities or agencies. Whether the information is fabricated or not, in most federal cases this information could still be used in the prosecution process whether it's directly or indirectly used. Meaning it could be used for relevant conduct at sentencing, or it could be used against the accused at his or her trial.

Now I have given you an overview of the steps in the criminal process and to be specific. I want to once again give you an outline, so you fully understand these steps:

1. **Arrested**: someone seized by legal authority and taken into custody.

2. **Arraignment:** where the court has three purposes: (1) to establish the identity of the accused; (2) to inform the accused of the charges against them; and (3) to allow the court to hear the plea of the accused whether guilty or not guilty.

3. **Bail:** is a deposit of money, property or some assurance of the accused that they will appear for court dates or trial at the time and date specified by the court.

4. **Preliminary hearing**: federal court does not always conduct a preliminary hearing in all criminal cases. Preliminary hearings are typically held when a defendant is charged with a federal offense and is being held in

custody or released on bail. However, a preliminary hearing is not mandatory in every case.

- The purpose of a preliminary hearing is to determine whether there is enough evidence for the case to proceed to trial. The prosecution must show probable cause that a crime was committed and that the defendant committed it.

- Preliminary hearings in federal courts are like one would be held in a state court proceeding and most of these types of hearings will be held within 14 days of the initial appearance of the accused /defendant. Keep in mind that if you are not awarded a bond, you have a right to petition the court for an appeal to set bond on your behalf in the appeals court that governs your district federal court.

Initial Plea

The initial plea where you plead not guilty when you first get arrested and brought into court. Which in most cases when an attorney appointed that will be the first plea. The attorney would advise the accused to enter a not guilty plea because pleading guilty during this stage can ruin the accused entire case especially if they are not guilty of the allegations presented against them in federal court.

The law does not tell you this, based on my experience I will. If you are not guilty, meaning if you did not commit the crime charge against you. You should not plead guilty just because you're going to receive a deal for less term of imprisonment, probation or fine for your freedom.

There are many individuals sitting in prison or in jail who have pleaded guilty to an offense/ crime that they claimed they did not commit. Once you plead guilty you lose your gun rights, (Second Amendment rights to the United States constitution). You lose your voting rights, and you lose your application right to remain in this country if you are an illegal alien from another country.

These rights will not be restored other than the voting rights for the residents of this country.

Pleading Guilty

In federal courts, nearly 98% of criminal cases are resolved through plea bargains according to the American Bar Association. This means that most convictions come from defendants pleading guilty rather than going to trial. Make sure you're offered enough information through your discovery of your Brady and your Jinx material to make an informed decision on how you want to pursue your case.

Brady Material: This refers to evidence that is favorable to the defendant in a criminal case, which the prosecution is required to disclose under the *Brady v. Maryland* (1963) ruling by the U.S. Supreme Court. This includes:

- Exculpatory evidence (evidence that may prove the defendant's innocence).
- Impeachment evidence (evidence that may discredit a prosecution witness).

Failure to disclose *Brady* material can lead to a conviction being overturned.

Giglio Material: "Giglio material" comes from *Giglio v. United States* (1972). This requires prosecutors to disclose any evidence that may affect the credibility of a government witness, such as:

- Prior inconsistent statements.

- Deals or promises made to witnesses in exchange for testimony.
- Any history of dishonesty or misconduct by a witness.

Both *Brady* and *Giglio* materials are crucial for ensuring a fair trial and protecting defendants' rights.

Jencks Material refers to statements and reports made by government witnesses that are in the possession of the prosecution, which must be disclosed to the defense after the witness has testified on direct examina**tion** at trial. These materials are crucial for **impeaching the credibility of government witnesses**, allowing the defense to cross-examine using prior statements. The Jencks Act governs the production of these materials.

Key Provisions of the Jencks Act – 18 U.S.C. § 3500:

1. **When Disclosure is Required:**
    - Only **after a government witness has testified** on **direct examination**.
    - The defense can then request **any statement** the witness made that relates to the subject of their testimony.
2. **What Qualifies as a "Statement"?**

    - A **written statement** made by the witness and signed or adopted by them.
    - A **recording or transcription** that is substantially verbatim.
    - A **grand jury testimony** of the witness.

3. **What Happens After the Request?**
    - The court inspects the materials and orders production of relevant statements.
    - If the government refuses to produce the material, the **court can strike the witness's testimony** or declare a mistrial.

Purpose and Importance:

The Jencks Act strikes a **balance between fairness and trial efficiency**:

- Ensures that the defense can **challenge witness credibility**.
- Prevents **early disclosure** that might endanger witnesses or impede investigations.

Note: The Jencks Act only applies to **government witnesses** in **criminal cases**—not civil cases.

Relation to Brady and Giglio:

- **Brady v. Maryland** (1963) requires **pretrial disclosure** of **exculpatory evidence**.

- **Giglio v. United States** (1972) extends Brady to include **impeachment evidence** (e.g., deals, promises).
- Unlike Brady/Giglio, **Jencks is not pretrial**—it's **triggered only after testimony begins**.

Now let's focus on the plea stage and other information that might be very interesting and important to the Accused Criminal Defendant.

Examples of Why You Should Not Plead Quilty to a Crime You Did Not Commit

Carol Ann Bonds v. United States 572 U.S. 844 (2014) is a case that stems from a domestic dispute between Ms. Carol Ann Bonds and her friend who was having an affair with Ms. Bonds' husband and got pregnant.

After becoming aware of the situation and finding a means of retaliation, Ms. Bonds, who had some kind of skill and knowledge to make chemicals, planted chemicals on her friend's door handles and car handles and things that she knew the woman might have to touch going in and out of her home.

The chemicals ruined the skin on the lady's hands. The authorities were informed, and Ms. Bonds was arrested on state offenses that were later turned over to the federal courts for prosecution.

The feds took up the offense and they used a statue that had similar context but was not the same as what the state's offense said was committed by Ms. Bonds.

Carol Ann Bonds went to trial after her attorney challenged the indictment statute under the Tenth Amendment of the United States Constitution. His challenge was based on the fact that the charge in the indictment was inconsistent with the actual crime she had committed.

The Court basically ignored her challenge because it was not normal during this point in time to make this type of challenge in a federal criminal case.

Ms. Bond presented the same challenge on direct appeal, which upheld the district court decision. Finally, after she had spent years incarcerated and making the same challenge, the United States Supreme Court granted Ms. Bonds relief and her case was sent back to the appeals court with instructions to allow her to make that challenge under the Tenth Amendment to the U.S. Constitution.

SEE: The **Tenth Amendment** of the U.S. Constitution states: "The powers not delegated to the United States by the Constitution, nor prohibited by it to the States, are reserved to the States respectively, or to the people."

While the Tenth Amendment itself does not specifically deal with criminal indictments, it reaffirms the principle of federalism—leaving powers not explicitly granted to the federal government to the states. Criminal indictments, however, are more directly addressed by other parts of the Constitution.

Supreme Court Case Validating Indictments

One critical Supreme Court case that validates and affirms the need for a grand jury indictment in federal criminal cases is **Hurtado v. California (1884).**

In **Hurtado v. California**, the Supreme Court ruled that the right to an indictment by a grand jury in the federal system, as guaranteed by the Fifth Amendment, does not apply to the states under the Fourteenth Amendment. This decision recognized that while the federal government must use a grand jury indictment in felony cases (as per the Fifth Amendment), the states can choose to use alternative charging methods, like a preliminary hearing, to charge individuals with crimes. However, for federal charges, the indictment process remains a requirement.

Challenging an Indictment

A criminal defendant in a federal case has the ability to challenge the indictment both during and before trial. The **Federal Rules of Criminal Procedure (FRCP)** specifically provide mechanisms for challenging indictments.

1. **Federal Rule of Criminal Procedure 12(b)**: This rule allows a defendant to file a motion to challenge the indictment, including on the grounds of insufficiency or defects in the charging document.

- **Rule 12(b)(3)** allows a defendant to raise challenges to the indictment, such as:
    - The failure to state an offense.
    - Defects in the indictment (e.g., lack of jurisdiction, improper venue, or failure to properly charge the offense).
    - Other legal defects in the way the indictment was presented.

  A defendant can file such a motion **before trial**, and if the motion is not raised in a timely manner, the right to challenge may be waived.

2. **Motion to Dismiss an Indictment**: Under Rule 12(b)(3)(B), a defendant can move to dismiss an indictment if it fails to state an offense or if there are other significant procedural issues. For example, if the indictment is flawed or does not properly specify the alleged crime, the defendant can request that the court dismiss the case before proceeding to trial.
    - **Rule 12(b)(3)(B)**: "The defendant may raise by pretrial motion any defense, objection, or request that the court can determine without a trial of the general issue."
3. **Pre-Trial Motions**: The defendant may also file pre-trial motions under **Rule 12(b)(2)** of the Federal Rules of Criminal Procedure, challenging the legal sufficiency of the

indictment, such as arguing that the indictment does not properly charge the crime.

- **The Tenth Amendment** doesn't directly address criminal indictments, but it upholds the principle of states' rights, leaving the federal powers to handle criminal procedures at the national level.
- The **Fifth Amendment** guarantees the right to a grand jury indictment for federal felonies.
- **Hurtado v. California (1884)** is a key Supreme Court case validating the federal grand jury indictment process.
- **Federal Rule of Criminal Procedure 12(b)** provides a criminal defendant with the ability to challenge an indictment on various grounds before trial.

Ms. Bonds' attorney saw that there were some discrepancies between the state charges and the federal charges against Ms. Bonds. The state charge was actually right based on the law. The federal charge was not; therefore, once the challenge was complete, Ms. Bonds went to the Supreme Court a second time, and it overturned her case. The charge that the government had was not factually based on the elements that were needed to coincide with the state charge and that would have actually been applicable to what Ms. Bonds had actually committed criminally. Therefore, Ms. Bonds was granted her liberty.

Ms. Bonds' case set precedents because before she won there had not actually been many published cases that made such challenges to the jurisdiction of the indictment. When an indictment fails to allege a proper offense that is legally justified under federal statutes enacted by the United States Congress, it may be defective. The indictment itself is what gives the federal court jurisdiction to prosecute a criminal defendant.

See: Federal Rules of Criminal Procedure, **Rule 7 - Indictment and Information**

1. The Indictment or Information

- **Rule 7(a)** states that an **indictment** is required for **felony** charges in federal court. For **misdemeanors**, charges may be brought by either an **indictment** or an **information** (a written accusation).
- **An indictment** is a formal accusation of a crime that is usually presented by a grand jury after investigating the case.
- **An information** is a formal charge made by a prosecutor without a grand jury indictment. This is more common in

misdemeanor cases or some other criminal matters where a grand jury is not required.

2. The Content of the Indictment

- **Rule 7(c)** specifies that an **indictment** must:
  - State the **official title** of the offense being charged.
  - **Set forth the nature** of the offense and the essential elements of the crime in enough detail to allow the defendant to understand the charge and prepare a defense.
  - Include a **plain, concise, and definite statement** of the essential facts constituting the offense charged.
- **The information** under Rule 7(d) must meet the same content requirements and must be signed by the prosecutor.

3. Amendment of the Indictment

- **Rule 7(e)** allows for the amendment of an indictment or information. It states that the court can permit an indictment to be amended **before trial** if no additional substantial prejudice to the defendant will result from the amendment. If an amendment occurs **after trial** has begun, the court must determine whether the amendment is necessary to ensure the defendant is not unfairly prejudiced.

4. Filing and Service

- **Rule 7(f)** indicates that the indictment must be filed with the court and served on the defendant. The **defendant** is then **notified** of the charge they are facing, and this is the first formal step in beginning a criminal case.

Summary of Key Points from Rule 7:

- **Indictment** is required for **felony charges** (grand jury indictment), but for **misdemeanors** charges can be brought via an **indictment** or **information**.
- An **indictment** must clearly state the offense, its essential elements, and enough factual detail to inform the defendant of the nature of the charge.
- The **court** has the discretion to **amend** an indictment **before trial**, provided it does not prejudice the defendant.
- **Information** is typically used in misdemeanor cases where no grand jury is required.

In summary, **Federal Rule of Criminal Procedure Rule 7** outlines the requirements for charging criminal offenses in federal court, including the need for an indictment for felony charges, the content requirements for indictments and information, and the procedures for filing and amending them.

Ms. Bonds committed a crime, but not the one she was accused of committing in federal court.

Now see the case of **Antonino Lyons (U.S. v. Lyons)**. Antonino "Nino" Lyons, a businessman from Coco, Florida, was wrongfully convicted in 2002 on federal charges, including drug conspiracy, carjacking, and counterfeit money and clothing, based on the federal prosecution's reliance on the testimony of a jailhouse snitch. His case garnered attention due to significant prosecutorial misconduct and the eventual dismissal of all charges against him.

A **jailhouse snitch** is a term used to describe an inmate who provides information to law enforcement or authorities about other prisoners, usually in exchange for some form of benefit. This could include a reduced sentence, improved living conditions, or other perks. The information provided by a jailhouse snitch is often about a fellow inmate's alleged criminal activities or confessions. They are placed in certain jails or fortunate enough to be in a position where they can gather information from other criminal defendants about their cases to use against them in their federal prosecutions.

Jailhouse snitches are sometimes viewed with skepticism because their testimony is often considered unreliable, especially when the snitch stands to gain something in return for their cooperation. As a result, their credibility can be questioned in legal proceedings.

What Happened

In 2001, Lyons was indicted by a federal grand jury in Orlando on multiple charges related to drug trafficking and other offenses. The prosecution's case heavily relied on the testimonies of 26 convicted felons, who claimed Lyons was involved in a large-scale cocaine distribution operation. Notably, there was no physical evidence—such as drugs, wiretaps, or surveillance—linking Lyons to these crimes. The witnesses received reduced sentences in exchange for their testimonies against Lyons.

In 2002, Lyons was convicted and faced a mandatory life sentence. However, it was later revealed that the prosecution had committed multiple violations, including withholding exculpatory evidence that could have impeached the credibility of key witnesses. These violations of Brady and Giglio obligations led to the court dismissing all charges against Lyons in 2004.

Prior to his arrest, Lyons was a legitimate entrepreneur. He owned a chain of clothing stores and was known in his community as a successful businessman. There is no credible evidence suggesting that his lifestyle was funded through illegal activities. The prosecution's case lacked physical evidence, and the allegations were primarily based on incentivized testimonies from convicted felons.

Lyons' case underscores the potential for miscarriages of justice when prosecutions rely heavily on uncorroborated testimonies and fail to disclose exculpatory evidence.

Lyons did not commit any crime at all, yet he sat in jail for more than a couple of years. Not only did he sit in jail, but he also went to trial and was convicted on all counts and was facing a life sentence .

All the evidence against him was false and the prosecution did not want to admit this, so they tried to give him a plea for less time or no time at all if he pled guilty.

Lyons pled not guilty, and pursued a jury trial. He lost almost everything he had except his integrity. The case was overturned after about four years, and a settlement didn't come until eight years later. Yes, this was a federal case, and I hope you don't think this was the first time this had happened. You can look this case up on the exonerated database.

Keeping You Informed

Whether you are detained or not, if you have been charged federally you should get an attorney. If you cannot afford an attorney, you should let the court know immediately so that one can be provided for you. If one has already been provided but they seem to have a conflict with you having the best defense that you feel is possible, you have to petition the court and express the conflict and request a new appointed attorney.

Check into the Criminal Justice Act (CJA), which is backed and authorized under the Sixth Amendment to the U.S. Constitution.

You should be appointed counsel, and all of your legal materials should be paid for by the government so that you can review them in order to make an informed decision about whether you wish to go to trial or plead guilty. This information also helps you to make an informed decision about whether to pursue a jury trial or one by a judge.

Your attorney should bring you every piece of information involved in your investigation that may jeopardize your freedom prior to you making any decision to do anything. Keep this in mind.

CJA Form 24, which is related to compensation and expenses for appointed counsel, may include notices informing the defendant and their attorney that the court will cover reasonable fees and expenses incurred for their defense, subject to the court's approval. Basically, this means that the accused can hire a private investigator to look for certain information that might be beneficial to their trial or case in general. So please take advantage of this because this might be an issue in your case.

To summarize:

- **18 U.S.C. § 3006A** establishes the right to court-appointed counsel for indigent defendants.
- **CJA Form 24** details the reimbursement procedures for appointed attorneys and may notify defendants that the court will pay for legal services when they cannot afford to do so themselves.

This ensures that defendants are informed that their defense and legal documentation (such as transcript fees or other court-related costs) may be covered under the CJA if they qualify as indigent.

Speedy Trial Rights

The accused has a right to a speedy trial, which in most cases is 90 days if the government doesn't file a motion for extension of time; however, they can and extend the time for very exceptional reasons.

This motion has to be granted by the court and sometimes these reasons are needed by the prosecution and for good reasons, such as to aid and assist the government in obtaining certain evidence. In a lot of cases the speedy trial process works against the government because they are not prepared to pursue a jury trial.

Many accused defendants do not know their speedy trial rights or do not have good counsel. They may miss the filing date or become frustrated with the process and plead guilty.

If you believe the government has no evidence or lacks the evidence they need to convict you, it is best to proceed under the speedy trial act which allows you to move forward.

The Speedy Trial Act is a critical piece of legislation in the United States that ensures criminal defendants have a right to a trial within a certain period of time, helping to prevent prolonged pretrial detention and undue delays. This law is particularly important in **federal criminal cases** because it enforces the constitutional right to a speedy trial, as guaranteed by the **Sixth Amendment** of the U.S. Constitution.

The **Speedy Trial Act of 1974, codified in 18 U.S.C. § 3161-3174**, mandates that the trial of a defendant in a federal criminal case must commence within a set time frame after the defendant is charged. This time frame is generally **70 days** from the date of the indictment or the defendant's first appearance in court, whichever comes later. However, the Act also outlines certain exceptions and conditions under which this timeline can be extended.

Key Provisions of the Speedy Trial Act:

1. **Time Limits for Trial:**

    - Under **18 U.S.C. § 3161(c)**, a federal trial must begin within **70 days** from the later of:
        - The filing of the indictment or information, or
        - The defendant's first appearance before a judicial officer.
    - The Act applies to all criminal trials in federal court.

2. **Excludable Time:**

    - Not all delays count toward the 70-day limit. There are several **exclusions** (called "excludable time") that extend the time before a trial must begin, such as:

  - Time needed for motions (pretrial motions, for example).
  - Delays caused by the defendant (e.g., continuances requested by the defense).
  - Time for a defendant to undergo medical evaluation or be mentally competent for trial.
  - Certain legal complexities or investigation delays.

- These exclusions are detailed in **18 U.S.C. § 3161(h)**.

3. **Sanctions for Violations:**

- If the trial does not begin within the prescribed 70-day period, and there are no valid exclusions, the case is **dismissed** with prejudice, meaning it cannot be refiled. This is a strong safeguard against prosecutorial delay.
- However, there can be exceptions if the delay was due to factors such as unforeseen circumstances or specific motions by either party.

Why the Speedy Trial Act Is Useful in a Federal Criminal Case:

1. **Protecting the Defendant's Rights:**

   The Speedy Trial Act ensures that defendants are not held in pretrial detention for an unreasonable period. This safeguards a defendant's **Sixth Amendment right** to a speedy trial, which aims to prevent prolonged uncertainty, stress, and potential loss of liberty.

2. **Reducing Court Backlogs:**

   The Act helps keep the judicial system efficient by imposing strict time limits on trials, which forces the government to move criminal cases forward without unnecessary delays.

3. **Preventing Prolonged Pretrial Detention:**

   The law helps to prevent an accused individual from being held in jail for too long before their trial. This is especially important for those who cannot afford bail and who may otherwise remain incarcerated while waiting for trial.

4. **Promoting Fairness:**

   - A speedy trial helps to preserve the **integrity of the case**, including witness testimony and evidence, which may degrade or become less reliable over time.

Important Case Laws and Interpretations:

Several key cases have shaped the interpretation and application of the Speedy Trial Act.

1. **Barker v. Wingo, 407 U.S. 514 (1972)**:

   While not directly related to the Speedy Trial Act (it was a Sixth Amendment case), **Barker v. Wingo** established a balancing test for determining whether a defendant's right to a speedy trial has been violated. The Court laid out four factors to consider:

   - The length of the delay
   - The reason for the delay
   - The defendant's assertion of their right to a speedy trial
   - The prejudice to the defendant caused by the delay

2. **United States v. Taylor, 487 U.S. 326 (1988)**:

   The **Taylor** decision clarified that **pretrial motions** (such as motions to suppress evidence) do not automatically toll the speedy trial clock, unless the motions are **"justifiably" complex**. Delays for routine motions will not count as "excludable time" under the Speedy Trial Act.

3. **Zedner v. United States, 547 U.S. 489 (2006)**:

   In **Zedner**, the U.S. Supreme Court ruled that a defendant's **waiver** of their right to a speedy trial must be **explicit** and made **knowingly and voluntarily**. The case emphasized the importance of ensuring that the defendant's right to a speedy trial is protected and that the waiver of that right is not presumed based on silence or inaction.

4. **United States v. Loud Hawk, 474 U.S. 302 (1986)**:

   In this case, the Court addressed the **"excludable time"** under the Speedy Trial Act, ruling that certain delays caused by the unavailability of defense counsel or the defendant's health could extend the trial date beyond the 70-day limit.

5. **United States v. Tinklenberg, 563 U.S. 647 (2011)**:

   The **Tinklenberg** decision clarified the application of the Speedy Trial Act's time exclusions. It emphasized that the **period during which a defendant requests a delay due to motions** could be excluded from the speedy trial calculation, even if those motions are not dispositive of the case.

The Speedy Trial Act provides structure and clarity in the federal criminal justice system. It ensures fairness and efficiency by:

- Protecting the rights of defendants to have a timely resolution of their case.

- Forcing prosecutors and defense attorneys to act promptly, preventing undue delays that could harm the defendant.
- Keeping the integrity of the case intact by preventing excessive delay, which could result in lost evidence or diminished witness credibility.

The **Speedy Trial Act** balances the need for efficient case management in the federal system with the constitutional rights of defendants, ensuring both the rights of the accused and the public's interest in timely prosecution are addressed.

It is not always good to pull the trigger on the speedy trial act to get out of jail or pursue the trial without all your necessary legal materials which can help mitigate the circumstances in your case or the case itself. Check out the information that follows and that I have already explained, but I want to reiterate it in more detail because it is very important that you are clear about this information in preparing yourself and your defense.

Plea and Trial Strategies

Prior to pursuing a jury trial or entering any plea agreement with the government, the accused's lawyer should file a motion on the federal rules of criminal procedure rule 16 to obtain all discovery materials that may consist of **DEA 6's, DEA 7's, and FBI 302'S**. Other materials from ATF may include items dealing with the controlled purchases and other activities of confidential informants' sources that participated in the state or the government's investigation. Their identities, if not redacted from materials, should be included.

DEA 6 Report of Investigation

- Purpose: Used by DEA agents to document events during an investigation—like surveillance, arrests, or interviews.
- Use in court: Often used to support affidavits or provide background in reports, but **not automatically admissible** as evidence.

DEA 7 Report of Drug Property Collected, Purchased, or Seized

- Purpose: Documents on the **handling of drug evidence**, including collection, weight, storage, and chain of custody.
- Use in court: Helps establish integrity **and chain of custody** for drug evidence.

FBI 302 Interview Summary

- Purpose: Documents what was said during an interview, **written by agents after the fact** (not verbatim).
- Use in court: Can be used to impeach a witness, but again, it's **not sworn testimony** or automatically admissible as evidence.

As mentioned above, your rights of discovery in criminal cases, unlike civil cases, are severely circumscribed apart from the government's Brady, Gigolo, and Jencks material.

Brady material or evidence is evidence that the prosecutor is required to disclose under this rule and includes any information favorable to the accused that may reduce a defendant's potential sentence or go against the credibility of an unfavorable witness or otherwise allow a jury to infer the defendant's guilt.

Brady material has three components: The evidence at issue must be favorable to the accused, either because it is exculpatory, or because it is impeaching; that evidence must have been suppressed by the State, either willfully or inadvertently; and prejudice must have ensued, concluded in the Strickler v. Greene Supreme Court 1999.

Giglio material is sometimes used to refer to any information pertaining to deals that witnesses in a criminal case may have entered with the government.

A **Giglio or Brady list** is a list compiled usually by a prosecutor's office or a Police Department containing the name and details of law enforcement officers who have sustained incidences of untruthfulness, criminal convictions, candor issues or some other type of issues placing their witness credibility into question. Therefore, most of this officer's information could be tainted and help free the accused. So be sure that you request this information, if available, from your lawyer because it should be made available to you.

Jencks material is a written or recorded statement made by a witness before a trial that the defendant can use or request to see in order to prepare for cross examination. The judge must, upon motion by the accused, order the government to disclose prior statements of its witnesses that are related to the subject matter of their testimony after or before each witness testifies on direct examination. See **Jencks v. U.S. 353 U.S. 657 (1957)**, in which Supreme Court held that the defendant is entitled to the pretrial access to statements made by the government witness.

All the information above is sufficient to enable the accused criminal defendant to make an informed decision on how he or she wishes to pursue their criminal case. Also, the scope of the investigation depends on this information for the attorney to determine whether the client is the target of the investigation and, if he or she is the target, whether immunity is available. It is the attorney's duty to inquire when they are aware that the accused does or does not wish to cooperate with the investigation. Only after all options have been fully explored can the accused make an informed decision about the future direction of their case.

If any of the above information is allowed in without being corrected prior to going to trial or after the trial has ended:

- Before closing arguments: If this is discovered in the course of trial, this could be used to request a mistrial.

- If this information happens to appear during the trial process and the Brady material is not presented along with the rest of the discovery to be reviewed by the accused before pleading guilty: This can effectively have a court not accept the accused plea if this is the case when asked if he or she was given an opportunity to review all discovery prior to making a decision to plead guilty.
- If the Court does not inquire or ask the accused, they should make it known that their

lawyer did not allow them the opportunity to review these materials prior to entering a plea.

An **informed decision** in the context of federal defense law typically refers to a situation where a defendant makes a decision about their case (such as whether to plead guilty, waive certain rights, or accept a plea deal) after being fully informed of their rights, the possible consequences, and the relevant facts surrounding their case. In essence, it means that the defendant has been provided with all the necessary information to make a decision that is both voluntary and intelligent.

Key Aspects of an Informed Decision:

1. **Right to Counsel**: The defendant must be informed of their right to consult with counsel and must make decisions about their case with the guidance of an attorney who is knowledgeable about the law and the specific facts of the case.

2. **Plea Decisions**: When a defendant is considering a plea bargain, the decision must be made with full knowledge of the consequences, including the possible penalties, the rights they are waiving (such as the right to a trial), and any collateral consequences (such as deportation for non-citizens).

3. **Waivers of Rights**: Informed decisions also apply to waivers of constitutional rights, such as the right to a trial, the right to remain silent, or the right to confront witnesses. A waiver must be done voluntarily, knowingly, and intelligently.

4. **Consequences**: Defendants must be made aware of the potential outcomes, such as sentencing guidelines, potential appeals, and the impact of their decisions on their future.

Key Case Law Explaining Informed Decisions:

Several important Supreme Court cases have addressed the importance of an informed decision in federal defense law, particularly in relation to guilty pleas, waivers of rights, and the right to effective counsel.

1. **Brady v. United States, 397 U.S. 742 (1970)**:

   This case involved a defendant who pled guilty after being informed of the potential penalties and the nature of the charges. The Court held that a guilty plea is valid if it is made voluntarily and with an understanding of the charges and potential consequences. In this case, the Court found that the defendant's plea was valid because he was aware of the consequences and the nature of the plea.

Ramifications: The decision established the principle that a plea must be "voluntary" and "intelligent," meaning that a defendant must understand what they are agreeing to before making a plea.

2. **North Carolina v. Alford, 400 U.S. 25 (1970)**:

   In this case, the Supreme Court allowed a defendant to plead guilty while maintaining his innocence, as long as the plea was made voluntarily and intelligently. The Court emphasized that a defendant's decision to plead guilty is valid even if it is done to avoid a harsher sentence, as long as the defendant understands the consequences of the plea.

   Ramifications: The decision reinforced the notion that a defendant must understand the nature of the decision they are making, including the potential for a longer sentence if they go to trial, but the plea still must be voluntary and informed.

3. **Hill v. Lockhart, 474 U.S. 52 (1985)**:

   This case clarified the standard for **ineffective assistance of counsel** during plea negotiations. The defendant claimed that he would not have pled guilty if he had been properly informed of the consequences of his plea. The Court held that to show ineffective assistance, the defendant must demonstrate that there is a reasonable probability that, but for counsel's errors, they would not have pled guilty and would have insisted on going to trial.

Ramifications: This case emphasized that a guilty plea must be based on **effective assistance of counsel**, meaning the defendant must have been informed about the likely outcomes and the rights they were waving.

4. **Padilla v. Kentucky, 559 U.S. 356 (2010)**:

   In **Padilla**, the Supreme Court held that defense attorneys have a duty to inform their clients about the **immigration consequences** of a guilty plea. In this case, the defendant pled guilty to a drug offense without being informed that this could lead to deportation. The Court ruled that the failure to inform the defendant of the deportation consequences amounted to **ineffective assistance of counsel**.

   Ramifications: This case expanded the scope of what it means for a defendant to make an informed decision. It clarified that **immigration consequences** (such as deportation) must be disclosed to the defendant, as these are significant factors in making an informed decision about whether to plead guilty.

5. **Faretta v. California, 422 U.S. 806 (1975)**:

In **Faretta**, the Supreme Court held that a defendant has the right to represent themselves in a criminal trial if they knowingly and intelligently waive their right to counsel. The Court emphasized that the decision must be informed, meaning the defendant must understand the disadvantages and risks of self-representation.

Ramifications: This case underscores the importance of ensuring that a defendant understands the consequences of waiving the right to counsel and the risks involved in representing themselves.

6. **Tollett v. Henderson, 411 U.S. 258 (1973)**:

   This case addressed a defendant's claim that his guilty plea was invalid because he was misinformed about the facts of his case. The Court held that once a defendant pleads guilty, they waive their right to challenge the constitutional validity of the charges (except in cases of ineffective counsel or coerced pleas). The Court emphasized that the decision to plead guilty must be based on the defendant's knowledge of the facts and the legal consequences.

   Ramifications: The ruling stressed that an informed decision involves understanding not just the law but also the facts of the case, and that a defendant who pleads guilty cannot later challenge those facts unless their plea was not made knowingly or was induced by ineffective counsel.

Why Informed Decisions Matter in Federal Defense Law

1. **Constitutional Rights Protection**: Ensuring that defendants make informed decisions helps protect their constitutional rights, including their right to effective counsel and their right to a fair trial. If defendants do not fully understand their options or the consequences of their decisions, their rights can be compromised.

2. **Avoiding Coerced or Unwilling Pleas**: The requirement for informed decision-making helps prevent coerced or unwilling guilty pleas, ensuring that a plea is made voluntarily and with an understanding of the implications.

3. **Preventing Legal Challenges**: Informed decisions are key to preventing later challenges to convictions. For example, if a defendant pleads guilty without understanding the consequences, they may later seek to overturn their conviction based on the claim that their plea was not valid.

An informed decision in federal defense law is a critical component of a fair and just criminal justice system. The case law highlighted shows the various ways courts ensure that defendants are making decisions with full knowledge of their rights, the consequences of their choices, and the implications of waiving those rights. Cases such as **Brady**, **Padilla**, and **Hill** underscore the importance of ensuring that decisions—whether to plead guilty, waive counsel, or go to trial—are made voluntarily, knowingly, and intelligently, and that a defendant is fully informed of the consequences involved.

What You Should Know About Search Warrants

Real talk. Do you know that most criminal defendants do not challenge the search warrant in a proper manner because they don't have a search warrant affidavit in their discovery materials? Without the search warrant affidavit there will be no search warrant.

A **search warrant affidavit** is a crucial document in the criminal justice system because it lays the foundation for a search warrant to be issued by a judge or magistrate. It provides the probable cause necessary to justify the search of a person's property or possessions. The affidavit serves as a written statement by law enforcement that outlines the facts and circumstances that lead them to believe a crime has been committed, and that evidence of that crime is likely to be found in the place to be searched.

The importance of the **search warrant affidavit** lies in its role in protecting a defendant's **Fourth Amendment rights**, which guard against unreasonable searches and seizures. The affidavit is meant to ensure that searches are not conducted arbitrarily or without adequate justification. In other words, it is a safeguard against unreasonable government intrusion into private matters.

Why Is the Search Warrant Affidavit Important?

1. **Probable Cause:**
The affidavit must demonstrate **probable cause**—a reasonable belief that a crime has been committed and that evidence of that crime will be found in the place to be searched. This is the constitutional standard required for law enforcement to obtain a search warrant. The affidavit should establish the basis of that belief by providing facts, observations, or reliable information from informants that support the claim.

2. **Judicial Oversight:**
Before police can conduct a search, the affidavit is submitted to a judge or magistrate, who reviews the information presented in the affidavit and determines whether there is probable cause to issue the warrant. This judicial oversight ensures that searches are not conducted without sufficient legal justification, offering a level of protection for citizens' rights.

3. **Transparency and Accountability:**
The affidavit serves as a transparent record of the law enforcement officer's reasoning for seeking the warrant. It provides accountability, ensuring that police actions are based on lawful principles and not on suspicion or arbitrary reasons.

4. **Limiting Scope of Search:**
A well-written affidavit limits the scope of the

search warrant. It specifies what law enforcement is looking for and where they are authorized to search. Without clear details, there is a risk of violating constitutional protections and conducting overly broad or intrusive searches.

Can the Search Warrant Affidavit be used to overturn a case or invalidate the warrant?

Yes, a search warrant affidavit can play a crucial role in **overturning a case** or **invalidating the warrant.** If the affidavit is found to be deficient or improperly constructed, it could lead to the **exclusion of evidence** obtained through that warrant.

Here are a few reasons why an affidavit could invalidate a warrant or lead to the overturning of a case:

1. **Lack of Probable Cause:**
   If the affidavit does not provide enough facts or detailed information to establish probable cause, the warrant may be invalid. For example, if the affidavit is based on vague or conclusory statements, or if it relies on unreliable sources without sufficient corroboration, a court may find the warrant to be invalid.

2. **False or Misleading Information:**
   If an officer intentionally or recklessly includes false information in the affidavit, or omits

critical facts that would affect the probable cause determination, the warrant could be challenged. The **Franks v. Delaware** decision (1978) established that a defendant can challenge the validity of a search warrant if they can show that the affidavit contained false statements made knowingly or with reckless disregard for the truth, and that those statements were material to the finding of probable cause.

3. **Insufficient Detail in the Affidavit:** A search warrant affidavit must provide specific details about why the search is necessary and what evidence is expected to be found. If the affidavit fails to provide sufficient factual information and just relies on general or vague claims, it may be considered insufficient to justify the warrant.

4. **No Nexus Between Crime and Location:** The affidavit must show a **nexus** between the criminal activity and the place to be searched. If the affidavit does not demonstrate how the location is connected to the crime (for example, if it just speculates that evidence will be found somewhere without facts to support that claim), the warrant may be invalidated.

Fruit of the Poisonous Tree Doctrine

The **Fruit of the Poisonous Tree Doctrine** is a legal principle that holds that evidence obtained from an illegal search or seizure (such as an invalid warrant) is inadmissible in court. The doctrine is based on the idea that if the initial search or seizure is unlawful (the "poisonous tree"), any evidence obtained as a result of that action (the "fruit") should also be excluded.

Key Aspects of the Fruit of the Poisonous Tree Doctrine:

1. **Illegal Searches or Seizures:** If a search or seizure is carried out without a valid warrant, or if the warrant is found to be invalid, any evidence obtained as a result of that unlawful action is considered "tainted" by the illegal action. This evidence cannot be used in the prosecution's case.
2. **Exclusionary Rule:**
   The doctrine is closely related to the **Exclusionary Rule**, which bars the use of evidence that was obtained in violation of the Fourth Amendment. Under the Exclusionary Rule, evidence obtained through an illegal search or seizure is generally inadmissible in a criminal trial.
3. **Attenuation Doctrine (Exception to the Rule):**
   There are exceptions to the Fruit of the Poisonous Tree Doctrine. One of the main exceptions is the **attenuation doctrine**, which

allows evidence to be admissible if the connection between the illegal search and the evidence is sufficiently distant or attenuated. For example, if law enforcement conducts an illegal search but later discovers the same evidence through an independent source, the evidence may still be admissible because it was not directly obtained through the illegal search.

4. **Independent Source Doctrine:**
   The **independent source doctrine** allows evidence to be admitted if it was discovered through a source independent of the illegal search or seizure. For example, if law enforcement learns about the evidence from a legitimate and independent investigation, the evidence may not be excluded, even if it was initially discovered during an illegal search.

5. **Inevitable Discovery Rule:**
   Under the **inevitable discovery rule**, evidence obtained from an illegal search may still be admissible if the prosecution can show that the evidence would have been discovered through legal means anyway. This means that if law enforcement can prove that the evidence would have been inevitably found regardless of the illegal search, the evidence can be used.

Case Law Related to the Fruit of the Poisonous Tree Doctrine

1. **Wong Sun v. United States, 371 U.S. 471 (1963):**

   This case established the Fruit of the Poisonous Tree Doctrine. The Supreme Court held that evidence obtained as a result of an illegal arrest was inadmissible in court because it was "fruit" of the illegal action. The Court emphasized that the exclusionary rule applies not only to evidence directly obtained from illegal actions but also to any evidence derived from them.

2. **Silverthorne Lumber Co. v. United States, 251 U.S. 385 (1920):**

   In this case, the Court ruled that not only the documents obtained through an illegal search were inadmissible but also any copies of those documents made later (the "fruit" of the poisonous tree). The Court set the groundwork for the Fruit of the Poisonous Tree Doctrine.

3. **Nix v. Williams, 467 U.S. 431 (1984):**

   This case solidified the **inevitable discovery rule**. The Court ruled that evidence obtained through an illegal search could still be admissible if law enforcement could show that the evidence would have inevitably been discovered by lawful means.

A **search warrant affidavit** is critical in federal defense law because it serves as the foundation for the search warrant itself. If the affidavit lacks probable cause or contains false or misleading information, it can lead to the invalidation of the warrant, and any evidence obtained from an illegal search can be excluded under the **Fruit of the Poisonous Tree Doctrine**. This doctrine is a safeguard against illegal government conduct, ensuring that evidence obtained through unlawful means cannot be used in court. However, exceptions like the **inevitable discovery rule** or the **independent source doctrine** can sometimes allow such evidence to be admissible if certain conditions are met.

Did you know that a search warrant expires, and if it's executed after the time or date of expiration that the search is considered illegal under the law?

See: U.S. Supreme Court case ***United States v. Jones, 565 U.S. 400 (2012)***. In this case, law enforcement officers obtained a warrant to install a GPS tracking device on Antoine Jones's vehicle. However, they installed the device **after** the warrant had expired and **outside** the jurisdiction specified in the warrant. The Supreme Court held that this constituted an unlawful search under the Fourth Amendment.

Key Legal Principles

1. **Expired Warrants Render Searches Unlawful**: Executing a search warrant after its expiration date violates the Fourth Amendment. In *Jones*, the GPS device was installed after the warrant had expired, making the search unauthorized.
2. **Physical Trespass and Privacy Violation**: The Court emphasized that physically intruding on private property to gather information constitutes a search. In this case, attaching the GPS device without a valid warrant was a physical intrusion that violated Jones's reasonable expectation of privacy.
3. **Good Faith Exception Not Applicable**: The "good faith" exception, established in *United States v. Leon*, 468 U.S. 897 (1984), does not apply when officers act without a valid warrant or outside its scope. In *Jones*, the officers' actions were not protected by this exception because they did not adhere to the warrant's terms.

Executing a search warrant after its expiration date, or outside its authorized scope, violates the Fourth Amendment. Evidence obtained from such a search is typically inadmissible in court. The *Jones* case underscores the importance of strict adherence to warrant requirements to protect individuals' constitutional rights.

Jones came out from under life sentences base on the Supreme Court's Ruling in his Case. Due to the GPS device being place outside of the time period, which is presented on a Warrant.

Basically, what I'm pointing out is that the accused criminal defendant should always challenge the search warrant based on the search warrant affidavit if they have any doubts that an error might have occurred during their prosecution.

There have been cases where the confidential informer (CI) already had the drugs on them when they lied about being sold drugs from a targeted residence, and the CI was never searched properly by law enforcement conducting surveillance before they went to the location. Some CIs later said that they didn't make the sale to the person who was the target of the investigation; they did go to the house and made a sale but to someone who didn't reside at that residence and just happened to be there conducting illegal business. Those statements made the CI uncredible and the search warrant was found illegal on probable cause.

See: **United States v. Leon, 468 U.S. 897 (1984)**

Case Overview:

In United States v. Leon, the U.S. Supreme Court addressed the issue of a search warrant based on an affidavit that contained **false information**

provided by a confidential informant. Although the Court ultimately upheld the exclusionary rule, it also recognized the **"good faith" exception** for law enforcement acting on a warrant issued by a judge.

Facts:

In **Leon**, law enforcement officers obtained a search warrant based on the information from a confidential informant. The informant was not known to be untrustworthy, but the affidavit later turned out to have **insufficient factual basis** to establish probable cause. Specifically, the affidavit relied on vague statements from the informant, and the magistrate judge who issued the warrant did not scrutinize the affidavit properly.

Court's Ruling:

Although the Supreme Court ultimately ruled that the **exclusionary rule** (the rule preventing the use of evidence obtained illegally) applied in the case, it also introduced the **good faith exception**. The Court held that even if the search warrant was based on a flawed affidavit, the evidence could still be used if the officers acted in **good faith** and believed the warrant to be valid.

However, the Court also acknowledged that if it could be shown that the affidavit relied on untruthful statements by a confidential informant, and the officers did not have a good faith belief in the validity of the warrant, the evidence would be excluded.

Impact:

- **United States v. Leon** clarified the **"good faith exception"** to the exclusionary rule. Even if a search warrant is based on an affidavit that contains false information from a confidential informant, law enforcement officers may still be able to use the evidence if they acted in good faith. However, this exception does not apply if the affidavit was clearly based on false or misleading information.
- The case highlights the importance of the accuracy and truthfulness of the information provided in a search warrant affidavit. If false information is included, the **Franks hearing** procedure may allow a defendant to challenge the validity of the warrant and the resulting evidence.

Both **Franks v. Delaware** and **United States v. Leon** emphasize the importance of the truthfulness and reliability of information, including from confidential informants, when law enforcement seeks a search warrant. **Franks v. Delaware** specifically allows defendants to challenge search warrants based on false or misleading information, including that provided by informants. While **United States v. Leon** established the good faith exception, it also reinforced that untruthful statements by an informant can invalidate a warrant and result in the exclusion of evidence.

Rule 11

Once again, I want to reaffirm some information about pleas and certain types of pleas for those individuals who feel the necessity to accept responsibility and plead guilty in their federal prosecution.

Under **Federal Criminal Procedures Rule 11** you have different types of pleas you can enter that could affect your case in different ways. Under this rule the court does not have to accept your plea; they can reject it and make you go to trial. However, 90% of the time, especially in federal court, you don't have to worry about that. But what you do have to worry about is **rule 11(c)(1)(c)**.

This is a rule that the court allows the accused to enter into a plea agreement in exchange for giving up all of their rights. Meaning that if a new law comes out and it's retroactive (meaning it applies to defendants who got sentenced in the past) and it now reduces sentences, for some reason the motion that the accused would usually file to reduce their sentence would not be allowed in most cases for rule 11(c)(1)(c) plea agreements.

If the accused wishes to enter into a guilty plea without a written agreement, that is his or her choice. If the government intervenes and states that this is the only plea that they will accept, then the accused should at least ask your attorney why.

These plea agreements are contracts. Once signed, the obligations of the agreement must be honored by the court. If the accused agrees to plead guilty and give up certain rights, such as the right to appeal to a higher court or a right to file a collateral motion (which is a motion that you file after you have been convicted and incarcerated or adjudicated on the case itself), then that's a right you have given up or waived based on a written plea agreement.

The government anticipates that somewhere down the line, when the accused has been convicted and incarcerated, they will try to find a way to reduce or mitigate their sentence. Therefore, these plea agreements are written up so that the defendant does not have an opportunity to reduce their sentence or overturn their conviction later down the line. A written plea agreement will prevent that.

Some of these plea agreements will actually request that the defendant give up their appeal rights, Freedom of Information act rights (which is under 552a), and their motion to file reduction of sentence under the 3582(c). So, when a new law is passed, they forfeit the right to make a filing even if the new law had the authority to change the defendant's sentence.

See: Freeman v. United States, 564 U.S. 522 (2011). In this case, the Court held that a defendant who entered into a plea agreement under Federal Rule of Criminal Procedure 11(c)(1)(C) could be eligible for a sentence reduction under 18 U.S.C. § 3582(c)(2) if the Sentencing Guidelines range applicable to the defendant's case was subsequently lowered.

Background

William Freeman pleaded guilty to multiple charges, including possession of crack cocaine, under a Rule 11(c)(1)(C) plea agreement, which stipulated a specific sentence. After his sentencing, the Sentencing Commission amended the Guidelines to reduce the sentencing range for crack cocaine offenses. Freeman sought a sentence reduction under § 3582(c)(2), but the lower courts denied his request, reasoning that his sentence was based on the plea agreement, not the Guidelines.

Supreme Court's Decision

The Supreme Court reversed the lower courts' decisions. The plurality opinion, authored by Justice Kennedy, concluded that a sentence imposed pursuant to a Rule 11(c)(1)(C) plea agreement could be "based on" the Sentencing Guidelines if the agreement was expressly tied to the Guidelines range. Justice Sotomayor concurred in the judgment, providing controlling opinion under the Marks rule. She emphasized that if a plea agreement is expressly based on a Guidelines sentencing range, and that range is subsequently lowered by the Sentencing Commission, the defendant is eligible for a sentence reduction under § 3582(c)(2) .

Key Takeaway

The Court's decision in Freeman established that defendants who enter into Rule 11(c)(1)(C) plea agreements are not categorically barred from seeking sentence reductions under § 3582(c)(2). Eligibility depends on whether the plea agreement was expressly based on a Sentencing Guidelines range that was later amended.

The accused person that is guilty and knows their rights and wrongs should plead guilty if they feel that is the right thing to do, unlike the innocent people who have been placed in circumstances that demanded that they plead guilty. Their concerns may have been many: being found guilty, adverse publicity, harm to their families, the possibility of an unfair sentence, the expense of attorneys and pursuing trial, being financially ruined. Their attorney may advise against such a decision; however, that choice is always the defendant's to make.

There are also instances where the accused will be willing to admit to certain aspects of the crime but not to others. Then your attorney must find a charge contained within the accusatory instrument, complaint information or indictment that is agreeable to all the parties as the basis for negotiation of a plea agreement. The government might agree and then all your legal actions could be settled with an appropriate term of incarceration or probation.

Whether you the accused, decide to pursue a jury trial, or take a guilty plea, this information should guide or help you make the right choice. At least it should clarify your options and make you more aware of your criminal charges and the choices that you will have to make. The opportunity to choose the best route to set or settle your criminal case often depends on multiple factors such as the specific circumstances of the case, the available evidence, and the goals of the defense. It's important to consider all legal options, and to pick one with which you can live.

Be mindful that if you decide to entertain the thought of a guilty plea agreement tendered by the government, you still have the right to negotiate once you receive notice from your attorney.

If you entertained and entered a plea agreement, but think that later down the line, prior to being sentenced, you may change your mind, you can always ask your attorney to file a motion to withdraw your plea. If given good enough reasons, the court will hold a hearing which is called an evidentiary hearing and bring out the facts that the accused alleged for withdrawing their guilty plea. Here are some notable cases where defendants sought to withdraw their guilty pleas:

- **United States v. Lawrence Benedict**: In this federal case, defendant Lawrence Benedict filed a motion to withdraw his guilty plea, citing multiple reasons including claims of innocence, newly discovered exculpatory evidence, prosecutorial misconduct, ineffective assistance of counsel, and the impact of prescription medication on his judgment. **See:** WIRED
- **United States v. Gardner**: The First Circuit Court of Appeals held that Gardner was entitled to withdraw his plea after the government withdrew from the plea agreement based on an alleged breach by Gardner. The court considered factors such as the voluntariness of the plea, the timing of the withdrawal request, and potential prejudice to the government. **See:** Criminal Legal News

If the accused has entered a plea, been sentenced to certain term of imprisonment, and is not satisfied, they can withdraw their guilty plea. Withdrawing of your guilty plea after sentence is under **rule 33.12 of criminal procedure** which states: after sentence is pronounced the judge should allow the defendant to withdraw a plea of guilty whenever the defendant upon a timely motion for withdrawal provides that withdraw is necessary to correct a manifest injustice. During this time the defendant has to provide information of why he or she wishes to withdraw their plea. Here are several reasons that are usually used when the accused federal defendant withdraws their guilty plea.

1. Ineffective assistance of counsel
2. Lack of legal counsel
3. Plea was entered without defendant's consent.
4. Defendant was not psychologically confident to plead guilty.
5. The strength of the defendant's case has risen.
6. Defendant was manipulated or threatened.

These are just some examples of the reasons that have been used in the federal courts by defendants wishing to withdraw their pleas.

The rule 11 plea agreement is a binding plea agreement entered into by the government and the accused for a certain sentence. When the defendant pleads guilty to a specific criminal charge in the agreement under this rule by the court, they are also agreeing to the terms of the agreement that once it is sealed by the court and established by the court, this agreement cannot be broken by anybody who enters into it or the court itself. Therefore, make sure that you bargain for what you want so that later on you won't regret entering into a guilty plea.

Before you enter into a plea agreement, do your due diligence on all that's available to you in a written plea agreement, because the government will set the terms of the agreement in favor of the government, not the accused.

In other words, a voluntary and an intelligent plea of guilty made by an accused person who has been advised by competent council may not be collaterally attacked. **See:** Mabry v. Johnson 467 U.S. 504 (1984)

Accepting Responsibility & Pleading Guilty Timely

In the federal criminal justice system, pleading guilty in a timely manner and accepting responsibility can significantly reduce a defendant's term of incarceration due to **sentencing guidelines** and **legal mechanisms** designed to reward defendants for showing remorse and cooperation with the legal process. Below are the key reasons why accepting responsibility and pleading guilty early in a case can led to a lighter sentence.

1. **Acceptance of Responsibility and the Sentencing Guidelines:**

In federal criminal cases, the **U.S. Sentencing Guidelines** provide a framework for judges to determine the appropriate sentence based on various factors, including the seriousness of the offense, the defendant's criminal history, and any mitigating or aggravating factors. One important mitigating factor is the **acceptance of responsibility**.

- **Guideline Reduction for Acceptance of Responsibility:**
  - **Section 3E1.1 of the Sentencing Guidelines** provides a specific reduction in a defendant's offense level if the defendant accepts responsibility for their conduct.

- The **maximum reduction** for acceptance of responsibility is **two levels** off the offense level, which can lead to a significantly lower sentencing range.

- **Timely Plea and Sentence Reduction:**
  - A defendant who pleads guilty **early** (before trial) is generally more likely to receive this reduction. If the defendant enters a **guilty plea** in a timely manner, they show that they are not delaying the proceedings and are taking responsibility for their actions, which is viewed favorably by the court.
  - In some cases, a defendant who enters a timely guilty plea and accepts responsibility might receive an additional **one-point reduction** under **Section 3E1.1(b)** if they assist the government by timely notifying authorities of their intention to plead guilty, thus saving the government time and resources. This can further reduce the sentencing guidelines range.

2. Plea Agreements and the "Substantial Assistance" Rule:

In certain cases, federal prosecutors may offer a **plea agreement** that can result in a reduced sentence. One way to secure a lower sentence is by cooperating with the government, particularly if the defendant provides **substantial assistance** in the investigation or prosecution of other individuals involved in criminal activities.

- **Section 5K1.1 (Substantial Assistance):**
  - **Substantial assistance** is when the defendant helps the government with important information or cooperation that leads to the prosecution or conviction of others. If the defendant provides substantial assistance, they may receive a **departure** from the sentencing guidelines under **Section 5K1.1**.
  - This assistance can result in a **significant reduction** in the sentence, depending on how valuable the information provided is. The earlier the defendant pleads guilty and begins cooperating, the more likely they are to receive this type of reduction.

3. "Fast-Track" Dispositions:

Some federal districts offer a **"fast-track"** plea program, particularly in immigration-related cases. These programs are designed to expedite the process for certain types of cases in exchange for a defendant's timely guilty plea.

- **Fast-Track Programs:**

- Under these programs, defendants who plead guilty early may be eligible for **sentence reductions** as part of a "fast-track" disposition. These reductions can be significant, often between **three to four levels** off the offense level, depending on the case and district.
- **Fast-track programs** are generally available for certain types of offenses, like illegal re-entry or certain drug offenses, and they provide a clear incentive for defendants to plead guilty quickly and accept responsibility.

4. Benefits of Pleading Guilty and Accepting Responsibility:

- **Reduced Sentence:**

  By pleading guilty and accepting responsibility early, a defendant can potentially reduce their sentence **significantly**. The **guideline reduction for acceptance of responsibility** and **possible cooperation with the government** can lower both the **offense level** and the **sentencing range**. This translates to a shorter prison sentence.

- **Avoidance of Trial and Trial Penalties:**
  - A **timely plea** can help a defendant avoid the full penalties associated with going to trial, where a conviction typically leads to

a harsher sentence. If the case goes to trial and the defendant is convicted, the judge may impose a sentence at the high end of the sentencing range because the defendant has not shown acceptance of responsibility. Additionally, a conviction after trial often involves a more lengthy and public process, which can result in a more severe sentence.

  - The **Federal Rule of Criminal Procedure 11** encourages judges to consider the defendant's decision to plead guilty early and accept responsibility, which may weigh in the defendant's favor at sentencing.

5. Sentencing Factors and Judicial Discretion:

In addition to the sentencing guidelines, judges in federal court have some degree of **discretion** in sentencing. Judges often take into account the defendant's **personal circumstances**, their **role in the offense**, and the **impact of their plea** on the broader justice system.

- **Acceptance of responsibility** is seen as an indicator that the defendant is less likely to reoffend and has shown remorse for their actions, which can influence the judge to impose a lighter sentence.
- A timely guilty plea and a defendant's cooperation with the court's process can also

influence the judge's decision-making, encouraging leniency in sentencing.

Key Case Law and Precedents:

1. **United States v. Booker, 543 U.S. 220 (2005)**:

   - This landmark Supreme Court case held that the U.S. Sentencing Guidelines are **advisory** rather than mandatory. While this gives judges more discretion, they are still encouraged to consider the guidelines and other relevant factors, including acceptance of responsibility, when sentencing a defendant. The decision in **Booker** reinforced the role of **mitigating factors** like guilty pleas in influencing the final sentence.

2. **United States v. Dunnigan, 507 U.S. 87 (1993)**:

   - In this case, the Supreme Court held that a reduction for acceptance of responsibility is warranted only if the defendant truthfully admits to their criminal conduct. The Court emphasized that a defendant who provides false statements during the plea process (i.e., lying about the facts of the case) is not entitled to the reduction.
   - **Dunnigan** made it clear that **genuine acceptance of responsibility**—not just a

guilty plea—was necessary to receive a reduction in sentencing.

3. **United States v. Pruitt, 482 F.3d 1004 (8th Cir. 2007)**:
   - The Eighth Circuit Court of Appeals held that a defendant who pleaded guilty and accepted responsibility for his actions was entitled to a downward departure in his sentence, as this was a **mitigating factor** that the judge was required to consider.
   - This case illustrates how **genuine remorse,** and a **timely guilty plea** can reduce a defendant's sentence by helping to satisfy the **sentencing guidelines** and enhancing the defendant's chances for a more lenient sentence.

Conclusion:

Pleading guilty in a timely manner and accepting responsibility in a federal criminal case can lead to **significant reductions** in a defendant's sentence. These reductions stem from **sentencing guidelines** that reward defendants for accepting responsibility and cooperating early in the legal process. The **two-level reduction** for acceptance of responsibility, along with the possibility of additional reductions for timely pleas or cooperation (e.g., substantial assistance to authorities), can significantly lower the defendant's offense level and thus reduce the length of incarceration. Additionally, a timely guilty plea helps avoid trial penalties and enhances the chances of receiving a more lenient sentence.

Strictly trial strategies:

If the accused decides to go to trial, this is one of the main types of motions you should consider having your attorney file on your behalf - a Bill of Particular.

Importance of a Bill of Particulars in a Federal Criminal Case

A **Bill of Particulars** is a formal, written request made by a defendant in a criminal case for a detailed explanation of the charges against them. It is an essential tool in federal criminal proceedings, primarily used to help the defendant understand the specific nature of the allegations, particularly in complex cases where the charges may be vague or overly broad.

Under **Federal Rule of Criminal Procedure 7(f)**, a defendant can file a motion for a Bill of Particulars to request more detailed information about the charges in the indictment. The importance of a Bill of Particulars can be broken down into several key functions:

1. Ensuring Adequate Notice:

A Bill of Particulars ensures that the defendant receives **adequate notice** of the charges they are facing, which is a key part of the **Sixth Amendment right to a fair trial**. It allows the defendant to understand the **specific facts** and **circumstances** that the prosecution will rely on, enabling them to prepare an adequate defense.

Without a Bill of Particulars, the indictment may leave a defendant unsure of what conduct they are being accused of, which could undermine their ability to mount an effective defense. This is especially important in cases with **complex charges**, such as conspiracy, fraud, or racketeering, where the defendant might not have all the facts about the specific acts or dates that are alleged to have occurred.

2. Preventing Surprise at Trial:

By providing clarity, a Bill of Particulars can help **prevent surprise** at trial. If the prosecution introduces new or unexpected evidence that was not outlined in the indictment, the defendant can request a continuance or argue for exclusion of the evidence due to lack of notice. It ensures that both parties—prosecution and defense—are on the same page regarding the **scope of the charges**.

For example, if a federal indictment alleges "a conspiracy to commit fraud" but fails to specify the dates, the individuals involved, or the specific fraudulent schemes, a Bill of Particulars can compel the prosecution to narrow down those allegations.

3. Protecting Against Double Jeopardy:

The Bill of Particulars also serves as a safeguard against **double jeopardy**, the constitutional protection against being tried for the same offense twice. By providing clear details of the charges, it ensures that the defendant knows exactly what conduct is being prosecuted, preventing the government from bringing new charges on the same facts in a subsequent trial.

4. Clarifying the Indictment:

In some instances, an indictment may be vague or **overly broad**. A Bill of Particulars can clarify ambiguities and specify the precise conduct, time frame, location, and other key details that the government intends to prove at trial. This specificity helps the defendant to prepare a defense, particularly if they need to gather evidence or call witnesses who can speak to specific events or facts.

Could a Criminal Defendant Be Granted a Mistrial Based on the Lack of a Bill of Particulars?

While the failure to grant a Bill of Particulars does not **automatically** result in a mistrial, it could be grounds for a **motion for a mistrial** if it can be shown that the defendant's ability to prepare a defense has been significantly hindered due to the lack of specificity in the charges.

A defendant may argue that without adequate details about the charges, they were not able to make informed decisions about trial strategy, which could lead to **prejudicial surprise** or **misleading evidence** being introduced at trial. If it can be shown that the lack of a Bill of Particulars led to unfair prejudice or compromised the defendant's right to a fair trial, the court could consider granting a mistrial or ordering a **continuance** to allow the defendant to better prepare.

That said, courts tend to prefer addressing these issues by ordering a **more detailed indictment** or an **amended Bill of Particulars** rather than immediately declaring a mistrial, as a mistrial is a drastic measure.

Cases Involving the Bill of Particulars:

1. **United States v. Clardy, 408 F.2d 1306 (9th Cir. 1969)**

   Facts: In this case, the defendant argued that the indictment was vague, and that the prosecution failed to provide sufficient detail about the charges. The defendant requested a Bill of Particulars to clarify the charges, but the trial court did not grant the request.

Ruling: The Ninth Circuit Court of Appeals held that the failure to provide a Bill of Particulars could be a valid ground for a reversal if it significantly impeded the defendant's ability to prepare for trial. The court emphasized that a Bill of Particulars is an essential tool to ensure fairness, and that lack of detail could hinder the defendant's ability to mount a proper defense. Although the court did not grant a mistrial here, it underscored the importance of providing adequate notice of the charges.

2. **United States v. Brimley, 529 F.2d 103 (6th Cir. 1976)**

   Facts: In this case, the defendant was charged with conspiracy to commit fraud, but the indictment was vague. The defendant requested a Bill of Particulars, arguing that the lack of specificity would leave them unable to properly defend against the charges. The trial court denied the motion.

   Ruling: The Sixth Circuit Court of Appeals ruled that the failure to grant a Bill of Particulars was an **abuse of discretion**, as the defendant was entitled to know the details of the charges to properly prepare a defense. The court found that the **lack of specificity** in the indictment could lead to unfair surprises, and **the defendant was prejudiced** as a result. The court reversed the conviction and remanded for a new trial, emphasizing the significance of a Bill of Particulars in ensuring fairness in criminal cases.

3. **United States v. Rios, 511 F.2d 1293 (9th Cir. 1975)**

   Facts: The defendant was charged with participating in a drug conspiracy. The indictment was not clear about the specific acts or individuals involved. The defendant requested a Bill of Particulars, but the trial court denied the request, and the defendant went to trial under the vague indictment.

   Ruling: The Ninth Circuit Court of Appeals held that the failure to provide a Bill of Particulars in a case where the indictment was vague and lacked sufficient detail was **error**, as it affected the defendant's ability to prepare a defense. The court also acknowledged that the failure to grant a Bill of Particulars could potentially lead to **prejudicial surprise**, and the **defendant was entitled to notice** of the specific charges. The court ordered the case to be reversed and remanded for a new trial with adequate notice of the charges.

The **Bill of Particulars** is an essential mechanism in federal criminal cases that helps ensure a defendant's right to a fair trial. It provides **clarity** and **specificity** about the charges, preventing **surprise** at trial, and safeguarding the defendant's ability to prepare a meaningful defense. While the failure to grant a Bill of Particulars does not automatically result in a mistrial, it can lead to **prejudicial error** if it affects the defendant's ability to mount a defense or creates **unfair surprise** at trial.

Courts have held that if the lack of a Bill of Particulars significantly impedes the defendant's trial preparation or leads to unfair prejudice, a conviction can be **overturned** or a new trial ordered. Cases like **United States v. Clardy**, **United States v. Birmley**, and **United States v. Rios** illustrate how important this tool is in maintaining fairness in criminal proceedings. While a mistrial may not always be granted, the court may **remand the case for a new trial** if the lack of specificity impacts the integrity of the trial process.

In the process the government has exposed its hand and the accused can opt out and enter a plea or pursue a new trial with ammo to shoot their shot once again. 12 in the box. Next, let's look into the motion in limine.

What is a Motion in Limine in Federal Court?

A **motion in limine** is a legal request made by a party (either prosecution or defense) to a court **before the trial begins** in order to exclude certain evidence from being presented to the jury during the trial. The primary purpose of this motion is to prevent the introduction of potentially prejudicial, irrelevant, or improper evidence that could unfairly influence the jury or harm the defendant's case. In federal criminal cases, a motion in limine can help both

Prosecution and defense ensure that the trial proceeds in a fair manner by addressing issues related to evidence before it is presented in court.

In the context of **federal criminal cases**, a motion in limina could be used by a **defendant** to ask the judge to exclude evidence that may violate their **rights** or be **inadmissible** under the Federal Rules of Evidence. These motions are often used to exclude evidence such as **prior criminal convictions**, **hearsay**, **irrelevant character evidence**, or **improper expert testimony**.

How Could a Motion in Limine Help the Criminal Defendant?

A **motion in limine** can help a **criminal defendant** in several ways:

1. **Exclusion of Prejudicial Evidence**: It can prevent the introduction of evidence that could unfairly prejudice the jury against the defendant. For example, evidence of a defendant's prior criminal record or allegations of uncharged crimes could create unfair bias in the jury's mind.

2. **Ensuring Fair Trial**: By excluding evidence that is irrelevant or unreliable, a motion in limine helps ensure that the trial is based on only the appropriate and legally admissible evidence. This promotes a fairer trial and protects the defendant's constitutional rights.

3. **Limiting Unfair Character Evidence**: Criminal defendants are often concerned that the prosecution will attempt to introduce evidence that improperly suggests the defendant has a bad character or prior bad acts. A motion in limine can prevent the prosecution from introducing evidence that would unduly influence the jury's perception of the defendant.

4. **Preempting Hearsay**: Hearsay evidence—testimony or statements made outside the courtroom—can often be excluded from trial. A motion in limine can request the court to rule on the admissibility of hearsay evidence before trial, preventing a situation where hearsay testimony could be introduced unexpectedly.

5. **Controlling Expert Testimony**: In criminal cases, expert testimony can sometimes be used inappropriately or without sufficient qualifications. A motion in limine can be used to exclude experts whose opinions may be unreliable or irrelevant.

6. **Protecting Against Unfair Legal Arguments**: A motion in limine can also address issues related to improper legal arguments, such as attempts by the prosecution to argue the defendant's guilt based on factors not related to the evidence presented.

Examples of How a Motion in Limine Could Benefit a Criminal Defendant

1. United States v. Williams, 385 F.3d 118 (2d Cir. 2004)

Case Overview: In **United States v. Williams**, the defendant was facing charges related to the distribution of narcotics. The government intended to introduce evidence of the defendant's past convictions for similar offenses to show a pattern of behavior.

Motion in Limine: The defendant filed a motion in limine to prevent the government from introducing evidence of his prior convictions. The defense argued that this evidence would unfairly prejudice the jury and violate the defendant's rights under Federal Rules of Evidence Rule 404(b), which prohibits the introduction of character evidence to prove a defendant's conduct.

Ruling: The court agreed with the defendant's motion in limine and excluded the prior convictions from evidence. The court noted that while such evidence might be admissible in certain circumstances, it could unfairly suggest that the defendant had a criminal propensity, thus leading the jury to improperly convict him based on past conduct rather than the evidence in the case at hand.

Benefit to Defendant: By excluding the prior convictions, the court ensured that the defendant would be judged based on the facts of the current case, not on his past criminal history, which could have unfairly influenced the jury.

2. United States v. Mendez, 16 F.3d 537 (7th Cir. 1994)

Case Overview: In **United States v. Mendez**, the defendant was charged with drug trafficking offenses. The prosecution sought to introduce a confession made by the defendant during a police interrogation. However, the confession had not been made voluntarily, and there were questions about whether the defendant's rights had been violated.

Motion in Limine: The defense filed a motion in limine to exclude the confession, arguing that it had been obtained through coercion and was not admissible under **Miranda v. Arizona**, 384 U.S. 436 (1966), which requires that a suspect be informed of their rights before making a confession.

Ruling: The court ruled in favor of the defendant and excluded the confession. The court determined that the defendant had not been informed of his rights and that the confession was coerced, which violated the defendant's constitutional rights.

Benefit to Defendant: By excluding the coerced confession, the defendant was protected from having an involuntary statement used against him at trial. This ruling ensured that the evidence presented was legally obtained and that the defendant's rights were upheld.

3. United States v. Chagra, 701 F.2d 354 (5th Cir. 1983)

Case Overview: In **United States v. Chagra**, the defendant was involved in a high-profile conspiracy case involving murder for hire. The prosecution sought to introduce certain pieces of evidence, including prior statements from co-conspirators that implicated the defendant.

Motion in Limine: The defense filed a motion in limine to exclude the statements made by the co-conspirators on the grounds that they were **hearsay** and did not fall within the exceptions provided by the **Federal Rules of Evidence**.

The defense argued that these statements should not be admitted into evidence without the ability to cross-examine the witnesses who made them.

Ruling: The court agreed with the defense and ruled that the co-conspirator statements were inadmissible because they did not qualify under the rules of hearsay exceptions, particularly because they lacked the necessary foundation for reliability.

Benefit to Defendant: The motion in limine effectively excluded the out-of-court statements that could have implicated the defendant, preventing unfair and unreliable evidence from being used against him.

4. United States v. Thornton, 801 F.2d 1281 (4th Cir. 1986)

Case Overview: In **United States v. Thornton**, the defendant was accused of a robbery. The prosecution intended to introduce evidence of a prior robbery that the defendant had allegedly committed, which the prosecution argued demonstrated a pattern of criminal behavior.

Motion in Limine: The defendant filed a motion in limine to exclude the prior robbery evidence, arguing that it was not relevant to the current charges and would unfairly prejudice the jury by making the defendant appear guilty based on prior bad acts.

Ruling: The court ruled in favor of the defendant and excluded the prior robbery evidence. The court determined that introducing this evidence would be overly prejudicial under **Federal Rule of Evidence 404(b)**, which prohibits the use of prior acts to prove a defendant's character or criminal propensity.

Benefit to Defendant: The ruling protected the defendant from being convicted based on prior crimes rather than the current charges. It ensured that the jury's judgment would focus on the actual evidence in the case, not on assumptions about the defendant's character.

A **motion in limine** is a powerful tool in federal criminal cases that helps ensure the fairness of a trial by excluding prejudicial, irrelevant, or inadmissible evidence. For criminal defendants, these motions can serve as a safeguard to prevent improper evidence—such as prior bad acts, coerced confessions, or unreliable hearsay—from influencing the jury.

As seen in cases like **United States v. Williams**, **United States v. Mendez**, and **United States v. Chagra**, motions in limine have been successful in protecting defendants from unfair legal arguments, improper evidence, and violations of their rights. By seeking to exclude certain evidence before the trial begins, defendants can strengthen their position and ensure that the trial is conducted based on legally obtained and relevant evidence, which ultimately helps safeguard their constitutional rights to a fair trial.

What is 404(b) Evidence?

Federal Rule of Evidence 404(b) governs the admissibility of certain **"other acts" evidence** in federal criminal trials. Under this rule, evidence of a defendant's prior crimes, wrongs, or other bad acts is **not admissible** to prove the defendant's character or propensity to commit the crime charged in the current case. This is often referred to as "propensity evidence." The reasoning behind this exclusion is that people may be judged unfairly if the jury is led to believe that someone who committed a crime in the past is more likely to have committed the crime currently charged.

However, **Rule 404(b)** does allow such evidence to be admissible **for other purposes**—if it is relevant to issues like:

- **Motive**: To show why the defendant may have committed the crime charged.
- **Intent**: To prove the defendant's intent to commit the crime, especially if the defendant's state of mind is at issue.
- **Knowledge**: To show that the defendant had knowledge of certain facts or circumstances.
- **Opportunity**: To show that the defendant had an opportunity to commit the crime.

- **Preparation**: To show that the defendant took steps to prepare for the crime.
- **Plan or Scheme**: To show that the defendant was engaged in a consistent or elaborate plan or scheme that links prior acts to the present charges.

How Can 404(b) Evidence Affect a Criminal Defendant?

404(b) evidence can have a profound impact on a defendant's case, particularly because the introduction of such evidence can severely **prejudice** the defendant in front of the jury. If the jury learns that the defendant has committed similar crimes in the past, they may assume that the defendant is guilty of the current charge because they have a "propensity" for criminal conduct. This can undermine the fairness of the trial, especially when the evidence is not directly relevant to the crime at hand.

Some ways **404(b) evidence** can affect a criminal defendant include:

1. **Prejudice**: The jury may focus more on the defendant's past actions rather than the current charges, potentially leading to a conviction based on past behavior.
2. **Distraction**: The introduction of irrelevant prior bad acts can distract the jury from

focusing on the actual evidence related to the case at hand.

3. **Assumptions about Character**: Evidence of prior crimes could lead the jury to believe that the defendant has a criminal character, even though such evidence is typically inadmissible under Rule 404(b).

Ways to Avoid 404(b) Evidence Being Used Against a Defendant

1. **Pre-Trial Motion to Exclude**: The most common method to prevent **404(b) evidence** from being used against a defendant is by filing a **motion in limine** before trial. This motion asks the court to exclude any prior bad acts or crimes that the prosecution intends to commit, arguing that such evidence is irrelevant or too prejudicial to the case at hand.

2. **Show Lack of Relevance**: A defendant's attorney can argue that the prior bad acts are **not relevant** to any of the factors under 404(b) (such as motive, intent, knowledge, or plan) and therefore should not be admitted. If the prosecution cannot show that the evidence falls into one of these categories, the court may rule to exclude it.

3. **Request for a Limiting Instruction**: If 404(b) evidence is admitted, the defense can

request that the judge give a **limiting instruction** to the jury. This would remind the jury that the prior bad acts are only to be considered for specific purposes (e.g., motive, intent) and not to determine the defendant's general character or propensity for crime.

4. **Challenge the Evidence's Admission**: The defense can challenge the **procedural aspects** of the 404(b) evidence, such as the failure of the prosecution to provide proper notice. According to **Rule 404(b)**, the prosecution must inform the defense of its intent to introduce such evidence before trial, and a failure to do so could be grounds for exclusion.

Cases Where 404(b) Evidence Was Introduced Unlawfully or Improperly

1. **Old Chief v. United States, 519 U.S. 172 (1997)**

   Case Overview: In **Old Chief v. United States**, the defendant, charged with being a felon in possession of a firearm, sought to prevent the prosecution from introducing evidence of his prior conviction (for assault causing serious bodily injury) under Rule 404(b) as part of the government's case in chief.

   Issue: The prosecution intended to use the prior conviction to prove the defendant's status as a felon. The defendant argued that introducing this prior conviction would unfairly prejudice the jury by suggesting he had a propensity for violence and criminal activity.

Ruling: The Supreme Court ruled in favor of the defendant. The Court emphasized that while **404(b) evidence** can be used in limited circumstances, the probative value of the prior conviction in establishing the defendant's felon status was minimal, and its prejudicial effect outweighed its usefulness. The Court concluded that the defendant's prior conviction was inadmissible and that its introduction would violate the defendant's rights to a fair trial.

Impact: This case demonstrates that 404(b) evidence, especially when it can prejudice the jury by suggesting a defendant has a propensity for criminal behavior, can be excluded if the prejudicial impact outweighs its probative value.

2. **United States v. LeMay, 260 F.3d 1018 (9th Cir. 2001)**

   Case Overview: In **United States v. LeMay**, the defendant was charged with sexual offenses. The prosecution sought to introduce evidence of prior sexual assaults committed by the defendant, arguing that it demonstrated the defendant's "motive" and "intent" in the current case.

Issue: The defense argued that introducing the evidence of prior sexual offenses was **unfairly prejudicial** and should be excluded under **Rule 404(b)**. The defense argued that the evidence would encourage the jury to convict the defendant based on prior conduct rather than the facts of the case.

Ruling: The Ninth Circuit Court of Appeals held that the prior acts were improperly admitted because the evidence was too prejudicial to be used to prove the defendant's motive and intent. The court ruled that the introduction of prior sexual offenses violated the defendant's rights to a fair trial.

Impact: The appellate court emphasized that **404(b) evidence** must be carefully scrutinized, and it cannot be admitted just to show that the defendant has a propensity for committing the offense. The case was remanded for a new trial without the improper 404(b) evidence.

3. **United States v. Green, 592 F.3d 1057 (9th Cir. 2010)**

   Case Overview: In **United States v. Green**, the defendant was charged with trafficking in stolen firearms. The prosecution sought to introduce evidence of the defendant's prior convictions for similar offenses under Rule 404(b) to demonstrate a "pattern of behavior."

Issue: The defense argued that this prior conviction evidence would improperly suggest the defendant had a propensity for criminal conduct and that its admission violated Rule 404(b). The defense also argued that the prior convictions were not sufficiently similar to the current offense to be relevant.

Ruling: The Ninth Circuit Court of Appeals ruled that the prior convictions should not have been admitted under Rule 404(b) because they were **not sufficiently relevant** to the current charges. The court found that the prior offenses were not sufficiently similar to the current charges to justify their introduction.

Impact: The appellate court's decision illustrates how **404(b) evidence** should only be admitted if the prior acts are sufficiently similar to the current charges and relevant to an issue like intent or pattern of conduct. The court found that the prior convictions were too dissimilar to be relevant, and their introduction likely caused **prejudice** against the defendant.

Rule 404(b) of the Federal Rules of Evidence plays a crucial role in determining whether a defendant's prior crimes or bad acts can be admitted in a federal criminal trial. While such evidence is generally inadmissible to prove a defendant's character or propensity to commit a crime, it can be introduced for specific purposes like showing **motive**, **intent**, **knowledge**, or **a pattern of behavior**.

However, when **404(b) evidence** is improperly introduced, it can severely prejudice a defendant and lead to an unfair trial. In cases like **Old Chief v. United States, United States v. LeMay**, and **United States v. Green**, courts have overturned convictions or ordered a new trial because **404(b) evidence** was used unlawfully or in a manner that violated the defendant's right to a fair trial.

To protect themselves, criminal defendants can file **motions in limine** to exclude such evidence before trial, demonstrate that the evidence is not relevant, or request limiting **instruction** to ensure that the jury does not use the evidence to unfairly assess the defendant's character.

This motion could avoid a lot of mishaps for the defense. For instance, 404 (b) of Criminal Rule of Procedures determines evidence upon this rule. It allows the government to introduce into the trial prior bad acts of the accused. For example, take the case where a middle-aged person had one or two prior drug convictions when they were 20 years old. The government would not want to use those convictions to show prior bad acts because they were too long ago to show that the defendant has a continuation of this type of criminal conduct. If criminal cases were more recent, say within the last four or five years and the accused was indicted on a drug trafficking conspiracy, the government would want to use the prior drug cases to show a continuation of bad acts by the accused.

Most times when the government introduces prior bad acts, the court has to explain to the jury that they are not supposed to find the defendant guilty based on those prior bad acts. But this is what's on the mind of a jury now: If they've done it once or twice before, what will make me think they wouldn't do it again? It would be common to think that way.

Motion For Acquittal

Once you pursue trial and it ends in a guilty verdict on all counts or maybe just on one count, then the accused has been convicted in a federal proceeding. Once the accused is convicted, the lawyer can file a motion for acquittal based on evidence that he thinks that should not have gone to the jury, or instructions that might have been prejudicial to your case, or whatever the case may be. But you are convicted. Now let's look at Rule 29.

What is Rule 29 of the Federal Rules of Criminal Procedure?

Rule 29 of the Federal Rules of Criminal Procedure addresses **motions for judgment of acquittal**. Specifically, it allows a **criminal defendant** to request the **court to acquit them** (i.e., dismiss the charges) when the evidence presented by the prosecution is insufficient to support a conviction. This motion can be made at the **close of the government's case** or after all evidence has been presented at trial.

In simple terms, **Rule 29** gives a defendant an opportunity to argue that the government has failed to meet its burden of proof and that no reasonable jury could convict based on the evidence presented.

The rule is important because it offers the defendant an opportunity to avoid a potentially wrongful conviction **before the case goes to the jury**. If granted, the court will enter a judgment of acquittal, which means the defendant is **acquitted of the charges** and the case is dismissed.

How Rule 29 Can Help a Criminal Defendant

Rule **29 motion** can significantly benefit a criminal defendant in the following ways:

1. **Preventing a Conviction**: If the prosecution has not presented enough **credible or sufficient evidence** to meet the required standard of proof, a **Rule 29 motion** can result in a dismissal of the charges before they are even presented to the jury. This avoids the risk of conviction altogether.
2. **Sufficiency of Evidence**: The defendant can argue that the government has **failed to establish a prima facie case** (i.e., the evidence is so weak that no reasonable jury could find the defendant guilty beyond a reasonable doubt). If the motion is granted, the case ends in the defendant's favor.
3. **Focus on Legal Deficiencies**: The motion can highlight legal deficiencies in the government's case, such as **lack of corroborating evidence**, **insufficient direct evidence**, or **failure to prove the essential elements** of the offense.

4. **Strategic Benefit**: Even if the motion is denied, filing Rule 29 motion provides the defendant an opportunity to preserve a legal challenge for potential **appeal**. This means that if the defendant is convicted, they can argue on appeal that the trial court erred in denying the motion for acquittal.

5. **Avoiding Jury Bias**: Rule 29 motion can be helpful if a defendant believes that the jury may be swayed by irrelevant or prejudicial evidence. If the court finds the evidence insufficient, the defendant may avoid the risk of a jury returning a conviction based on such evidence.

Examples of Cases Where Rule 29 Was Used Successfully

1. United States v. Acosta, 17 F.3d 160 (2d Cir. 1994)

Case Overview: In **United States v. Acosta**, the defendant was charged with **narcotics trafficking**. After the prosecution rested its case, the defendant filed a **Rule 29 motion** for a judgment of acquittal, arguing that the prosecution's evidence was insufficient to prove that he was involved in the drug trafficking conspiracy.

Ruling: The Second Circuit held that the **trial court properly denied** the motion. The court found that the evidence, including testimony from cooperating witnesses, was sufficient for a jury to reasonably conclude that Acosta was involved in the conspiracy. However, this case illustrates how Rule 29 motions are typically used when the defense believes that the evidence is weak or inconclusive.

While the defendant in this case did not prevail on the Rule 29 motion, the case shows that Rule 29 can be a useful mechanism for challenging the sufficiency of evidence and protecting the defendant's right to a fair trial.

2. United States v. Vargas, 577 F.3d 57 (1st Cir. 2009)Case Overview: In **United States v. Vargas**, the defendant was charged with **conspiracy to distribute cocaine**. The defense filed a Rule 29 motion for acquittal after the government presented its case-in-chief, arguing that the evidence was insufficient to prove the defendant's involvement in the conspiracy.

Ruling: The First Circuit reversed the district court's decision, finding that the evidence was insufficient to sustain a conviction. Specifically, the court noted that while there was some circumstantial evidence, there was no direct evidence linking the defendant to the cocaine trafficking operation. The defendant's motion for acquittal was granted.

Impact: This case highlights how Rule 29 motion can be a powerful tool in criminal defense. In this case, the court determined that the prosecution's evidence was insufficient, and the defendant was acquitted of the charges.

3. United States v. Gallo, 721 F.2d 1567 (11th Cir. 1983)

Case Overview: In **United States v. Gallo**, the defendant was charged with **racketeering and conspiracy**. After the prosecution rested its case, the defendant filed a Rule 29 motion, arguing that the evidence was insufficient to establish the **elements of the crimes** charged.

Ruling: The Eleventh Circuit upheld the trial court's decision to deny the Rule 29 motion. The court found that there was sufficient evidence, including witness testimony and physical evidence, to allow a reasonable jury to convict.

Impact: While the defendant ultimately did not prevail on the Rule 29 motion, the case demonstrates the importance of evaluating the sufficiency of evidence. Even when a motion is denied, it preserves the defense's ability to raise issues on appeal.

4. United States v. Yoon, 128 F.3d 1559 (10th Cir. 1997)

Case Overview: **United States v. Yoon** involved charges of **wire fraud**. The defendant filed a Rule 29 motion after the government presented its case, arguing that the prosecution's evidence was insufficient to prove the **intent** to defraud.

Ruling: The Tenth Circuit reversed the district court's decision to deny Rule 29 motion, finding that the evidence was insufficient to prove the defendant's intent to defraud. The court concluded that the evidence presented at trial did not meet the standard required for a conviction.

Impact: The reversal in this case demonstrates how **Rule 29** motions can be used to challenge the sufficiency of evidence related to key elements of a crime, such as intent, and can lead to a **judgment of acquittal** if the evidence is deemed insufficient.

Learning and understanding the sentencing procedures in federal court.

Once the accused gets convicted and the U.S. probation department completes a pre–sentence investigation report (PSI), the defendant will be brought back to court for sentencing, which could be a very confusing and tricky situation. Based on the proceedings themselves, prior to the court's sentencing date your lawyer and the government will have to file sentencing memorandums on the defendant's behalf and against considering the government's position. The government will be asking the judge for a certain amount of time based on what they believe the defendant should receive. Both motions will be ruled on during this phase of the sentencing.

In the PSI you will see the United States Guidelines being used to determine what base offense level, criminal history, and other enhancements or reductions that may be applied to the sentencing calculus. The criminal defendant sentencing calculation will be based on qualifications outlined in the guidelines' manual. The cases 2005 Booker versus United States and Blakely versus United States made the guidelines advisory. Prior to 2005 the guidelines were mandatory in any sentencing term of imprisonment that may have applied to the criminal defendant.

The government used to specify a certain range of imprisonment to the court and generally the court ruled within that range. The sentencing guidelines calculation used the defendant's criminal history level, base offense level, and any relevant conduct that was the issued and granted by the court during the sentencing phase.

After the 2005 Supreme Court rulings, that's no longer the case. Instead of the federal sentencing guideline manual being mandatory, it's only used as a measuring stick for the court to pronounce a sentence. The sentence might be in a range of the guidelines that is applicable to the defendant, or the judge can reduce or enhance a sentence they believe is justified based on 3553(a) factors which I shall explain later.

Prior to conviction, the person is just accused. After conviction, he or she becomes a criminal defendant. The following sections will deal with the defendant from a trail point of view.

Learning the U.S. Sentencing Guidelines

Overview of Chapter One of the U.S. Sentencing Guidelines Manual

Chapter One of the **U.S. Sentencing Guidelines Manual** serves as the foundational part of the guidelines, explaining the philosophy, structure, and general framework under which federal courts are to sentence criminal defendants. It provides specific instructions to ensure consistency, fairness, and proportionality in sentencing across the federal criminal justice system.

Below is a breakdown of the important principles and concepts typically found in **Chapter One**:

1. Purpose of the Sentencing Guidelines

The Sentencing Guidelines were created to promote uniformity in sentencing decisions. Before the guidelines were established, there was more variation in sentences from one court to another. The goal of the guidelines is to:

- **Promote fairness** by ensuring that similarly situated defendants receive similar sentences.
- **Avoid unwarranted disparity** in sentencing.
- **Provide clear and understandable rules** for both judges and lawyers.

- **Reflect the seriousness of the offense** and the defendant's criminal history.

2. Structure of the Guidelines

The guidelines are divided into **two primary components**:

- **Offense Level**: This is determined by the seriousness of the crime committed (e.g., whether it involved violence, drugs, or financial crimes). The offense level is increased or decreased based on factors such as the victim's vulnerability or the use of a weapon.
- **Criminal History**: This category takes into account the defendants' previous criminal convictions and their overall criminal history. More prior convictions typically result in a higher sentence.

The **Chapter 5 Sentencing Table** is part of the **U.S. Sentencing Guidelines**, which are used by judges to decide how long someone should be sentenced to prison or other types of punishment for committing a crime. The table helps make sure that sentences are fair and consistent across similar cases.

Step 1: Identify the Offense Level

First, the court looks at what crime the defendant committed and assigns it a **base offense level**. The offense level is a number that corresponds to how serious the crime was. For example, a serious crime like armed robbery would have a higher offense level, while a less serious crime, like shoplifting, would have a lower one.

Let's say our defendant is convicted of a **drug trafficking crime**. The court assigns this crime a base offense level of **30** (just an example).

Step 2: Add or Subtract Points for Specific Factors

The court then looks at any **specific factors** that might make the crime worse or better. These are things like:

- Did the defendant have a gun?
- Was the victim particularly vulnerable?
- Did the defendant cooperate with the police?

If the defendant gets points added because of aggravating factors (like using a weapon), their offense level might increase. Conversely, if they get points subtracted for mitigating factors (like showing remorse), their offense level might decrease.

For example, if the defendant helped the police during the investigation, the court might **subtract 2 points** from the offense level.

Step 3: Find the Sentencing Range

Once the offense level is decided, the court looks up that level on the **Chapter 5 Sentencing Table.** This table is a grid that shows how long a defendant should be sentenced to prison, depending on their offense level and criminal history.

The table has two parts:

- **Offense Level (Y-axis)**: This runs from 1 to 43, with 43 being the most serious.
- **Criminal History (X-axis)**: This shows the defendant's prior criminal record. If they have a lot of previous convictions, they'll have a higher criminal history score.

SENTENCING TABLE
(in months of imprisonment)

	Offense Level	Criminal History Category (Criminal History Points) I (0 or 1)	II (2 or 3)	III (4, 5, 6)	IV (7, 8, 9)	V (10, 11, 12)	VI (13 or more)
	1	0–6	0–6	0–6	0–6	0–6	0–6
	2	0–6	0–6	0–6	0–6	0–6	1–7
	3	0–6	0–6	0–6	0–6	2–8	3–9
Zone A	4	0–6	0–6	0–6	2–8	4–10	6–12
	5	0–6	0–6	1–7	4–10	6–12	9–15
	6	0–6	1–7	2–8	6–12	9–15	12–18
	7	0–6	2–8	4–10	8–14	12–18	15–21
	8	0–6	4–10	6–12	10–16	15–21	18–24
	9	4–10	6–12	8–14	12–18	18–24	21–27
Zone B	10	6–12	8–14	10–16	15–21	21–27	24–30
	11	8–14	10–16	12–18	18–24	24–30	27–33
Zone C	12	10–16	12–18	15–21	21–27	27–33	30–37
	13	12–18	15–21	18–24	24–30	30–37	33–41
	14	15–21	18–24	21–27	27–33	33–41	37–46
	15	18–24	21–27	24–30	30–37	37–46	41–51
	16	21–27	24–30	27–33	33–41	41–51	46–57
	17	24–30	27–33	30–37	37–46	46–57	51–63
	18	27–33	30–37	33–41	41–51	51–63	57–71
	19	30–37	33–41	37–46	46–57	57–71	63–78
	20	33–41	37–46	41–51	51–63	63–78	70–87
	21	37–46	41–51	46–57	57–71	70–87	77–96
	22	41–51	46–57	51–63	63–78	77–96	84–105
	23	46–57	51–63	57–71	70–87	84–105	92–115
	24	51–63	57–71	63–78	77–96	92–115	100–125
	25	57–71	63–78	70–87	84–105	100–125	110–137
	26	63–78	70–87	78–97	92–115	110–137	120–150
	27	70–87	78–97	87–108	100–125	120–150	130–162
Zone D	28	78–97	87–108	97–121	110–137	130–162	140–175
	29	87–108	97–121	108–135	121–151	140–175	151–188
	30	97–121	108–135	121–151	135–168	151–188	168–210
	31	108–135	121–151	135–168	151–188	168–210	188–235
	32	121–151	135–168	151–188	168–210	188–235	210–262
	33	135–168	151–188	168–210	188–235	210–262	235–293
	34	151–188	168–210	188–235	210–262	235–293	262–327
	35	168–210	188–235	210–262	235–293	262–327	292–365
	36	188–235	210–262	235–293	262–327	292–365	324–405
	37	210–262	235–293	262–327	292–365	324–405	360–life
	38	235–293	262–327	292–365	324–405	360–life	360–life
	39	262–327	292–365	324–405	360–life	360–life	360–life
	40	292–365	324–405	360–life	360–life	360–life	360–life
	41	324–405	360–life	360–life	360–life	360–life	360–life
	42	360–life	360–life	360–life	360–life	360–life	360–life
	43	life	life	life	life	life	life

Let's say the defendant's final offense level after adjustments is **30**, and their criminal history category is **III** (meaning they have a moderate criminal history).

Step 4: Look Up the Sentence

Now, the judge can look at the table and find the intersection of offense level **30** and criminal history category **III**. The table might show a **sentence range** of **97 to 121 months** (about 8 to 10 years in prison).

Example Summary:

- **Offense**: Drug trafficking (base offense level = 30)
- **Adjustments**: Subtracted 2 points for cooperation with authorities (final offense level = 28)
- **Criminal History**: Category III (moderate criminal history)
- **Sentence Range**: 78 to 97 months (about 6.5 to 8 years in prison).

Based on the Chapter 5 Sentencing Table, the judge would likely sentence the defendant to somewhere between 6.5 and 8 years in prison, depending on any other factors they consider. The sentencing table helps judges decide a fair prison sentence based on how serious the crime was and the defendant's history.

The Federal Sentencing Guidelines are rules judges use to determine appropriate prison sentences for federal crimes. These guidelines are divided into chapters, and **Chapter Two** is one of the most important because it covers **"Offense Conduct"**—that means the specific crime a person is being sentenced for.

Each type of crime is organized under a specific **Section** in Chapter Two, and every section has a code that looks like this: §2D1.1 or §2K2.1. These codes tell you exactly **how to calculate the base offense level for that crime.**

How the Sections Work:

- §2D1.1 → **Drug Offenses**
- §2K2.1 → **Firearm (Gun) Offenses**
- §2B1.1 → **Fraud and Financial Crimes**

Each section includes:

- A **Base Offense Level** (starting point for sentencing).
- **Specific Offense Characteristics** (things that make the sentence higher or lower).
- **Adjustments and Enhancements** (based on conduct like leadership roles or weapon involvement).

Example 1: Drug Offense – Cocaine Distribution

- **Guideline Section:** §2D1.1

- **Base Offense Level:** Depends on the drug type and quantity.
    - Example: If caught with **5 kilograms of cocaine**, the base level might start at **32**.
- **Enhancements:**
    - If a weapon was possessed during the drug offense, add **+2 points.**
    - If the person was a leader or organizer of the drug ring, add **+4 points.**

Final Offense Level Example:
Base Level 32 + 2 (gun) + 4 (leadership) = **Level 38**
This level determines the sentencing range in months using the Sentencing Table.

Example 2: Firearm Offense – Illegal Gun Possession

- **Guideline Section:** §2K2.1
- **Base Offense Level:**
    - Starts at **14** if the person simply possessed a firearm unlawfully.
    - If the person has prior felony convictions or the firearm was stolen, the level can increase.
- **Enhancements:**

    - If the gun was used in connection with another felony (like drug trafficking), add **+4 points**.
    - If the firearm was a high-capacity weapon or fully automatic, further increases apply.

Final Offense Level Example:
Base Level 14 + 4 (used in drug trafficking) = **Level 18**

Example 3: Fraud Offense – Bank Fraud

- **Guideline Section:** §2B1.1
- **Base Offense Level:** Starts at **7** for basic fraud.
- **Enhancements:**
    - Based on the **amount of loss** caused by the fraud:
        - Loss of $150,000 → Add **+10 points**.
        - Loss of $1 million → Add **+16 points**.
    - If the fraud involved 10 or more victims, add **+2 points**.
    - If the person used sophisticated means, add **+2 points**.

Final Offense Level Example:
Base Level 7 + 16 (loss amount) + 2 (sophisticated means) = **Level 25**

Key Takeaways for Readers:

- Chapter Two of the Guidelines tells you **what starting point to use for each crime** and how to add or subtract points based on case details.
- The **higher the final offense level, the longer the sentence**.
- This system applies to nearly every federal case, from drugs and guns to fraud and immigration crimes.
- Knowing these guideline sections can help you or your loved ones understand the sentencing exposure they face and how lawyers negotiate plea deals.

Together, the **offense level** and **criminal history** are used to calculate a **sentencing range**, which the judge uses as a starting point for determining the sentence.

3. Role of the Court and Judicial Discretion

Although the guidelines provide a sentencing range, the judge still has discretion within that range. Courts must consider the following factors when determining the final sentence:

- **The nature of the offense**: What exactly was the crime, how serious was it, and how harmful was it to society?
- **The defendant's personal characteristics**: This includes their background, mental health, and role in the offense. A defendant who has shown remorse or taken steps to rehabilitate themselves may receive a more lenient sentence.
- **The need to deter crime**: The judge will consider whether the sentence will help deter the defendant and others from committing similar crimes in the future.
- **The need to protect the public**: If the defendant poses a continued threat to public safety, this might influence the court to impose a harsher sentence.
- **The need for rehabilitation**: If the defendant shows potential for rehabilitation (e.g., through education or drug treatment), the judge might consider a sentence that facilitates their rehabilitation.

4. Departure and Variances from the Guidelines

While the guidelines are generally binding, there are provisions for **departures** and **variances** in certain cases. A **departure** occurs when a judge adjusts the sentence based on factors not covered by the guidelines. A **variance** is a broader adjustment, typically made if the judge finds that the recommended sentence does not serve the interests of justice. In both cases, the judge must explain the reasoning for deviating from the guidelines.

Some of the common reasons for departures or variances include:

- The defendant's **mitigating factors** (e.g., a mental health condition, or lack of intent to cause harm).
- **Aggravating factors** that were not fully considered by the guidelines.
- **Substantial cooperation** with law enforcement (such as testifying against co-defendants).

5. Sentencing Factors Considered by the Court

The court must also consider other factors when imposing a sentence:

- **Sentencing Enhancements or Reductions**: The guidelines may call for increases or decreases in the offense level based on certain aggravating or mitigating circumstances. For example, using a firearm during the commission of a crime could increase the sentence, while cooperating with authorities might reduce it.

- **Victim Impact**: The effect of the crime on the victim(s) is a factor. For instance, crimes involving significant harm to the victim (e.g., violent crimes, financial harm) could lead to higher sentences.
- **Acceptance of Responsibility**: If a defendant pleads guilty and takes responsibility for their actions, this may result in a reduced sentence.

6. Mandatory Minimum Sentences

In some federal cases, there are **mandatory minimum sentences** that judges must impose for certain offenses (such as drug trafficking or firearms violations). These sentences override the sentencing guidelines if the judge's calculated sentence is lower than the mandatory minimum.

7. Sentencing of Organizations

Chapter One also addresses the sentencing of **organizations** (such as corporations or other entities), which have their own guidelines and considerations. These often focus on the company's role in the crime and the steps it has taken to prevent future misconduct, including paying fines and making restitution.

8. Sentencing After Conviction

Once the judge has determined the sentence, the defendant may be:

- **Sentenced to prison** (with a set term or a life sentence in extreme cases).
- **Placed on probation** (typically for less serious crimes or after serving a portion of the prison sentence).
- **Ordered to pay restitution** to victims or fines as part of the sentence.
- **Given other conditions**, such as drug treatment, community service, or reporting to probation officers.

Chapter One of the U.S. Sentencing Guidelines Manual establishes the broad framework within which federal judges must work to determine sentences in criminal cases. It emphasizes **uniformity** while allowing **judicial discretion** in individual cases based on the specific circumstances of the offense and the defendant. The guidelines prioritize the principles of **deterrence, protection of the public, rehabilitation, and just punishment**.

Which states the court shall determine the kind of sentence and guidelines range as set forth in the guidelines under United States Code 3553 (a). by applying the provisions of this manual in the following order, except as specifically directed. One determines by 1B1.2 applicable guidelines range for the offense conduct charged in the indictment.

Chapter Two (Offense Conduct) is applicable to the offense of conviction. Each offense has a corresponding base offense level and may have one or more specific offense characteristics that adjust the offense level upward or downward. For instance, a criminal defendant gets a sentence for a gun he or she has been convicted of possessing. They are sentenced under 2K 2.1, which states the base offense level for a convicted felon in possession of a firearm also known as a 922(g) would face penalties under 924(a).

Another example: A criminal defendant sentenced for drugs trafficking, conspiracy or a possession with intent to sell or deliver would be sentenced under United States Sentencing Guidelines 2D1.1 for the base offense level attributed to the total amount of drugs presented in the PSI, a finding made by the United States Probation officer based on proffer letters, testimony of cooperating witnesses or physical evidence found or seized during the investigation of the criminal defendant.

A criminal defendant that gets sentenced for murder would be sentenced under 2A1.1. Basically, every provision in Chapter Two deals with the direct base offense levels unless the court decides to use a cross reference. For example, the murder might be a cross reference, and the accused was charged for a drug trafficking offense that carried a base offense level of 34. The calculation would be considered as it may be applied to the sentence. For Instance, someone can mention this information about a murder committed during the time of the accused conspiracy case. Then the base offense level would be level 43 for murder in the First degree.

In a document, a co-conspirator or anyone that is assisting the government can just mention someone who got murdered and that it was supposedly/allegedly done by the defendant or accused person. The government would accept the fact that the accused person may have caused the death of a person before he or she was indicted. Whether charged for the murder or not, the accused could still be sentenced for the crime based on relevant conduct information enhancements from the U.S. Sentencing Guidelines Manual, which comes in after entering a plea or a finding of guilt after trial.

The defendant can argue against it but based on the USSG 1b1.3 relevant conduct, it may be considered reasonable and foreseeable. The evidence does not have to be something tangible (i.e., physical); it could be evidence that's given by someone who has testified on the witness stand or who has given a proffer letter to an agent or the government stating that these events happened and that they witnessed them. Therefore, if someone said they witnessed the criminal defendant and did not hear this information from a third party, it's relevant conduct and it can be used in the sentencing calculus. The courts usually give the criminal defendant a higher base offense level and enhanced sentence under Chapter two unless the court decides to not use the Chapter two base offense level for the charged offense conduct and instead uses the base offense level for the cross reference like murder, which is under Chapter Two as well.

Learning about Relevant Conduct

In the context of federal criminal cases in the United States, relevant conduct refers to the broader set of criminal acts and activities that are considered in sentencing a defendant beyond the specific charges for which the defendant has been convicted. This concept is particularly important in the application of the United states sentencing guidelines which provide a framework for federal judges to determine the appropriate sentences for convicted defendants under the U.S. sentencing guidelines.

Relevant conduct includes not only the specific offense of conviction but also other relevant conduct that is part of the same course of conduct or common scheme or plan as the offense of conviction. This can encompass a range of criminal activities that are related to the convicted offense even if the defendant has not been formally charged or convicted of those specific acts. When the criminal defendant is sentenced in a federal court, a judge may consider relevant conduct in order to impose a sentence that reflects the defendant's actual criminal behavior and the harm caused by that behavior.

This allows for a more comprehensive assessment of the defendant's culpability and the impact of their actions. In the context of relevant conduct, the sentencing guidelines take into account factors such as quantity of drugs involved, the amount of financial loss, the number of victims affected and the leading roles in the criminal activity. These factors can result in adjustments to the sentencing range and potentially leading to a longer or aggravated sentence based on the totality of the defendant's criminal conduct. It's important to note that the determination of relevant conduct in federal cases can be complex and may involve legal arguments and evidentiary considerations.

Defense attorneys and prosecutors often engage in detailed discussions and present evidence to the court regarding the scope and the nature of relevant conduct during the sentencing phase of the criminal case.

In federal sentencing, **relevant conduct** refers to the actions, behaviors, and circumstances that are considered by the court when determining the appropriate sentence for a defendant convicted of a crime. Relevant conduct can include not only the specific offense for which the defendant was convicted but also other actions or offenses that are connected to the conviction, even if the defendant has not been charged or convicted for those specific actions.

Relevant conduct is crucial in the **U.S. Sentencing Guidelines**, which provide a framework for judges to determine the sentence in federal criminal cases. These guidelines are designed to ensure consistency and fairness in sentencing, though judges have discretion to adjust sentences based on the individual circumstances of each case.

The Accused person is not even aware of this before they enter guilty plea or pursue a jury trial. Therefore, the accused need to know now that this is a possibility, and a can occur if there is a possibility this information may exist at the time of their federal prosecution. The sad thing about it is you can't even prepare for it or do anything about it. But once it's implemented you can make the necessary challenges during the sentencing phase that the information is not reasonably foreseeable. See below:

Reasonably Foreseeable Challenges to Relevant Conduct

A defendant can challenge relevant conduct during sentencing by arguing:

1. Lack of Involvement or Knowledge

- **Argument**: "I wasn't involved in that part of the conspiracy," or "That was not reasonably foreseeable to me."
- **Example**: In a drug conspiracy, the defendant might argue they only trafficked 50 grams, not the 500 grams trafficked by co-conspirators.

2. Not Within the Scope of the Joint Criminal Activity

- **Argument**: The actions of others were outside the agreed-upon plan or were done independently.
- **Example**: A defendant may argue a co-conspirator's violent act was not in furtherance of the criminal scheme they jointly planned.

3. Lack of Proof by a Preponderance of the Evidence

- Relevant conduct must be proven by the government by a **preponderance of the evidence** (more likely than not).
- **Argument**: "The government hasn't proven I did that with enough evidence."
- Defendants can attack witness credibility, inconsistencies, or the lack of corroborating evidence.

How It Affects the Sentence

Successfully challenging relevant conduct can:

- **Reduce the base offense level** (especially in drug and fraud cases, where quantities drive the level)

- **Avoid enhancements** (e.g., for use of a weapon, bodily injury, number of victims, etc.)
- **Support a lower sentence** within or below the guideline range.
- **Influence a judge to vary from the guidelines** under **18 U.S.C. §3553(a)** factors.

In most cases, murder is a capital crime that has to be charged in the indictment or charging instrument, but not in federal cases, where the accused does not have to be indicted for murder like in most states' crimes. In federal court, the judge can use the murder as an enhancement to circumvent a murder charge itself. First the court would give you the base offense level for the drug amounts, because Chapter Two of the guidelines' manual says to do so. Then the court would come with the cross reference and use the murder guidelines which start out at life for a first-degree murder under level 43.

Key Components of Relevant Conduct in Federal Sentencing:

1. **Offenses that are Part of the Same Course of Conduct or Common Scheme or Plan**
    - When calculating a defendant's sentence, the court may consider crimes committed as part of the **same course of conduct** or a

common scheme or plan as the offense of conviction. This can include:

- o Other crimes committed during the same criminal episode.
- o Multiple offenses that share a similar purpose or motive, even if they occur over time or in different locations.

- For example, if someone is convicted of **drug trafficking**, and evidence shows they were involved in multiple drug deals that were part of the same trafficking operation, the court could consider those additional crimes in sentencing.

2. **Other Acts and Offenses (Related to the Conviction)**

- Even if the defendant was not charged with or convicted of specific acts, the court can still consider those acts if they are part of the defendant's **relevant conduct**. These may include:
  - o Acts that the defendant participated in but were not included in the formal charges.
  - o Offenses that the defendant committed but were not directly charged, such as additional drug transactions or violent acts related to the primary offense.

- Other uncharged offenses, provided that they can be proven by a preponderance of the evidence (i.e., more likely than not).

3. **Convictions that are Part of a Larger Criminal Activity**

- Sometimes, a defendant may have been involved in a broader criminal enterprise. If other convictions or offenses are tied to the primary crime, those may be considered relevant conduct. For example:
  - A **racketeering case** (RICO charge) could involve not only the primary racketeering activity but also other criminal acts like money laundering, bribery, or fraud that were committed by the defendant as part of the larger criminal scheme.
  - Even if the defendant is not convicted of every crime, the sentencing guidelines allow for the inclusion of all relevant conduct related to the broader criminal enterprise.

4. **Intent and Knowledge of the Offense**

- The defendant's **intent**, **knowledge**, or **recklessness** when committing the offense can influence relevant conduct. For example:

- If the defendant was **aware** of the broader criminal activity they were involved in, this could be factored in when considering the sentence.
- **Aggravating or mitigating factors**: Relevant conduct may include a defendant's motive, whether they acted with malice or deliberation, or whether they showed remorse.

5. **The Quantity of Drugs or Loss Amount**

   - In cases involving **drug offenses** or **fraud**, the court will often look at the quantity of drugs involved or the total amount of financial loss as part of the relevant conduct. Even if the defendant was convicted of a smaller amount, the court may consider evidence that they were involved in a larger operation.
     - For example, in drug trafficking cases, the defendant may be convicted of trafficking a smaller amount of drugs but could face a higher sentence if there is evidence that they were involved in trafficking much larger quantities.

6. **Victim Impact**

- In some cases, the **impact on the victims** may be considered relevant conduct. This could include:
    - **Financial loss** in fraud cases.
    - **Physical injury or harm** in violent crime cases.
    - **Psychological harm** in cases involving sexual assault, domestic violence, or other crimes where victims are impacted in ways beyond just the physical act.

How Relevant Conduct Affects Federal Sentencing

Relevant conduct plays a significant role in calculating a defendant's **sentencing guidelines range** (the range of imprisonment recommended by the Sentencing Guidelines), which is based on a variety of factors, including:

1. **Base Offense Level**: Each offense has a base offense level in the guidelines.
2. **Specific Offense Characteristics**: Certain factors, like the amount of drugs or the use of violence, can increase or decrease the offense level.
3. **Adjustments Based on Relevant Conduct**: The **total offense level** can be adjusted based on relevant conduct. For instance:

- If the defendant committed additional crimes that are connected to the primary offense, the offense level may be increased.
- If the defendant was less involved or played a lesser role in the broader criminal conduct, it might result in a **reduction** in the offense level.

4. **Guideline Enhancements or Departures**: The judge may apply specific enhancements (increasing the sentence) based on the defendant's actions or the harm caused, or they may depart from the guidelines in certain circumstances.

Example of Relevant Conduct in Sentencing:

- **Scenario**: Suppose a defendant is convicted of **possession with intent to distribute** a certain amount of cocaine. However, during the investigation, it is revealed that the defendant was also involved in a larger cocaine distribution operation, even though they were only charged for a smaller amount. The sentencing judge may consider the larger quantity of drugs in the **relevant conduct**, increasing the defendant's sentencing range under the guidelines.
- **Another Example**: A defendant is convicted of **wire fraud** for embezzling

money from a company. Even if they were only convicted for embezzling $100,000, if evidence shows that they were involved in a broader scheme that caused $1 million in losses, the court may consider the total $1 million loss as relevant conduct, leading to a higher sentence.

- **Relevant conduct** refers to the actions, crimes, and behaviors connected to a defendant's offense that may be considered by the court during sentencing.
- Relevant conduct includes **other crimes** committed as part of the same course of conduct, **uncharged acts** that are proven to be connected, and other factors like **victim impact**, **loss amount**, and **the defendant's intent**.
- The **Sentencing Guidelines** use relevant conduct to adjust the **offense level**, which determines the recommended sentence range, ensuring that sentencing reflects the defendant's full involvement in criminal conduct.

Relevant conduct should be illegal for the simple fact that, as I mentioned earlier, you can go to court for a drug conspiracy even though you're only charged for a drug trafficking offense in your indictment.

During the course of the sentencing phase, the United States probation officer and the United States Attorney can go inside this United States guideline manual and actually pick out things in the guidelines that could be applied to the defendant's base offense level based on information that they received through the course of their investigation.

For instance, the highest base offense level for a drug distribution charge - **2D1.1** for a drug trafficking charge or conspiracy charge - can only go up to a level **38** for the most drugs of any category under Chapter Two of the United States Sentencing Guideline. But the government can say that somebody testified or proffered information about a murder that took place within the last two or three years of this conspiracy and that the criminal defendant was involved in it. The accused who pleaded guilty or was found guilty now faces a term of imprisonment for a murder that was not charged in their indictment instead of just the conspiracy charge for drug trafficking.

The accused might have pleaded guilty and faced 17 years. After the PSR (also called a PSI) is issued and relevant conduct is factored into the sentencing range, that same criminal defendant now may face a sentencing calculation of 30 years because he or she was given additional levels in addition to their original sentencing calculation that was most likely quoted by their attorney prior to the actual sentencing proceedings. In some cases, the criminal defendant's guideline range goes up to life from a lower range that was first told to them prior to sentencing. If there is information concerning a murder or other types of crimes that may have been committed by the accused during the time of the conspiracy offense, or any crime the accused was originally charged for in the government's indictment against them, that same criminal defendant may face a substantial increase of time if the court uses a cross-reference base offense level. This happens during the sentence phase of the prosecution of a federal criminal defendant.

Proffer or testimony statements could be used in the sentencing calculation to substantiate facts for an alternate base offense level, not for the drug trafficking offense charged against the defendant but cross referenced for murder or other crimes which may expose the criminal defendant to a higher guidelines provision under the **USSG Chapter 5 A** sentencing table.

See: USSG 1B1.(B)(a) and the application notes which specify the same to this extent: that if there are two guidelines involved in a sentence calculation, that the court has the authority to use the highest one to give a base offense level.

In most cases the court uses the highest guidelines range whether it's the murder cross reference over the drugs base offense level or some other that is applicable. The drugs base offense level is always much lower than the murder cross reference or other provisions that could be used based on relevant conduct.

Relevant conduct does not have to be based on murder. Murder is just an example of how the courts add and use miscellaneous enhancements by utilizing the federal sentencing guidelines manual to manufacture a sentence that is much longer than a normal unenhanced sentence based on a regular guideline for the actual crime charged in the indictment.

Understanding § 3553(a) Sentencing Factors

What is 18 U.S.C. § 3553(a)?

18 U.S.C. § 3553(a) is a statute that guides federal judges when imposing a sentence after a defendant is convicted of a federal crime. It requires the court to impose a sentence that is **"sufficient, but not greater than necessary"** to meet the goals of sentencing.

Purpose of § 3553(a):

While the U.S. Sentencing Guidelines provide a recommended sentencing range, § 3553(a) allows judges to **vary upward or downward** based on specific circumstances of the case. This gives the court **discretion** to impose a sentence that fits both the offense and the individual.

The Key Factors Under § 3553(a):

Here are the main sentencing factors the judge must consider:

1. **Nature and circumstances of the offense and the history and characteristics of the defendant** *(§ 3553(a)(1))*
2. **The need for the sentence to:**
    - Reflect the seriousness of the offense
    - Promote respect for the law
    - Provide just punishment

- Afford adequate deterrence
- Protect the public
- Provide the defendant with needed educational or vocational training, medical care, or other correctional treatment *(§ 3553(a)(2))*

Example in Practice:

Case: A 22-year-old defendant pleads guilty to possession with intent to distribute heroin. **Guidelines Recommendation:** 120 months.

3553(a) Factors Considered by the Judge:

- **§ 3553(a)(1):** First-time offender, no prior record, grew up in poverty, got involved due to drug addiction.
- **§ 3553(a)(2)(D):** Completed drug rehab program before sentencing, shows genuine remorse, and wants to pursue vocational training.
- **§ 3553(a)(6):** Co-defendants in similar roles received 60–72 months.
- **§ 3553(a)(2)(A–C):** Public safety not a major concern; no violence or weapons involved.

Sentence Imposed: 60 months — a **downward variance** from the Guidelines based on the totality of the 3553(a) factors.

Why It Matters:

Understanding **§ 3553(a)** is crucial for advocacy during sentencing. It opens the door for arguments **beyond the cold numbers of the Guidelines**—including rehabilitation, family circumstances, youth, mental health, disparity, and more.

Let's break down how **rehabilitation**, **family support**, and **age** are used under § 3553(a) to argue for a **downward variance** in sentencing.

1. Rehabilitation – (§ 3553(a)(2)(D))

What the statute says:
The court should consider "the need... to provide the defendant with needed educational or vocational training, medical care, or other correctional treatment in the most effective manner."

How it works:
If a defendant shows genuine steps toward rehabilitation—such as completing drug treatment, gaining employment, or mentoring others—judges can consider that as a basis to reduce the sentence.

Example:
A defendant convicted of drug trafficking completes an intensive, court-approved rehab program and earns a GED while out on bond. The judge finds that the defendant is on the right

path and that prison time would stall this progress. The judge gives a 36-month sentence instead of the 60-month guideline.

2. Family Support – (§ 3553(a)(1))

What the statute says:
The judge must consider "the history and characteristics of the defendant."

How it works:
Strong family ties and community support can show the court that the defendant has a support system that lowers the risk of recidivism and increases the chance for successful reintegration.

Example:
A single mother convicted of fraud has no prior record, cooperated with authorities, and has primary custody of three young children. Her family and church offer supervision and support. The judge considers her role as a caregiver and the stability family support provides, sentencing her to probation with home confinement instead of prison time.

3. Age – (§ 3553(a)(1))

What the statute says:
Also part of the "history and characteristics of the defendant."

How it works:
Youth may suggest impulsiveness, capacity for change, and rehabilitation potential. Advanced

age may suggest lower risk of reoffending and health concerns, especially if the defendant poses no danger.

Examples:

- **Young Defendant (18 years old):** Sentenced for robbery but had no criminal history and was under the influence of older peers. The court finds his brain was not fully developed and that he's amenable to reform. The judge imposes a sentence below the guideline minimum to give him a second chance.
- **Elderly Defendant (65+):** Convicted of tax fraud. Due to health issues, low risk of recidivism, and the burden prison would place on a frail person, the judge imposes home confinement and supervised release instead of incarceration.

Bottom Line:

Under **§ 3553(a)**, these personal factors give judges **flexibility** to sentence based on **who the person is**, not just **what they did**. These arguments are powerful when supported by:

- Evidence (letters, certificates, treatment records)
- Testimony (family, counselors, mentors)
- A compelling sentencing memorandum

These procedures are followed when the criminal defendant gets convicted and has to file for relief challenging their conviction or sentence. Once they get back in court, if the court decides to resentence them this information is what puts the defendant in a position to get their sentence lowered or reduced to time served based on the judge's consideration.

Self-Help Strategies for the Accused

During the legal process as an accused criminal defendant, you have to take the time to condition yourself mentally and physically for this type of situation. You have to have emotional and logical support strategies for coping with the toll of being accused and maintaining your mental and physical well-being throughout the legal process.

Dealing with the emotional impact of incarceration and maintaining mental resilience throughout the legal process can be incredibly challenging. For individuals facing criminal charges and navigating the criminal justice system The combination of emotional strain, uncertainty, and the potential for a long period of incarceration can feel overwhelming. However, there are strategies and approaches that can help manage stress, maintain mental health, and cope with emotional challenges. Below are some ways to cope with and maintain mental stability in these circumstances:

1. Acknowledge and Accept Emotions

- Recognize Your Feelings: It's important to understand that feelings of fear, anger, sadness, frustration, and isolation are natural responses to being incarcerated and facing legal challenges. Acknowledging these emotions is the first step in managing them. Bottling up feelings can lead to increased stress and anxiety, so allow yourself to feel, but try not to get lost in those emotions.

- Practice Self-Compassion: Treat yourself with kindness during this difficult time. It's easy to be self-critical, especially in the face of legal trouble, but remember that this situation does not define your entire life. Practice self-compassion and recognize that you're doing the best you can under challenging circumstances.

2. Focus on What You Can Control

- Take Control of Your Daily Routine: While much of the legal process and life in jail or prison can feel beyond your control, there are elements you can manage. Develop a routine where you can focus on simple, productive activities like reading, writing, exercising, or learning a new skill. This will give you a sense of control and purpose.

- Focus on Preparation: In the legal process, preparation is key. Work closely with your lawyer, review case details, and ask questions to understand what's happening at each stage. This can help reduce feelings of helplessness and make you feel more empowered.

3. Build and Maintain Support Networks

- Stay Connected to Family and Friends: Maintaining communication with supportive loved ones can be a lifeline. Regular contact with family or close friends through phone calls, letters, or visits helps you feel grounded, loved, and understood. These connections can alleviate feelings of isolation and provide emotional support.

- Seek Support from Fellow Inmates: If you are incarcerated, consider reaching out to others who may be facing similar challenges. Sharing experiences with others can foster a sense of community and lessen feelings of loneliness.

- Consider Therapy or Counseling: Many correctional facilities offer counseling services. Talking to a mental health professional, whether a therapist or counselor, can help you process your emotions and learn strategies for coping with stress and anxiety. If formal therapy is not available, peer counseling programs may also provide support.

4. Develop Coping Strategies for Stress

- Mindfulness and Meditation: These practices can significantly reduce anxiety and stress. Mindfulness involves being present and aware of your thoughts and feelings without judgment. Meditation, even in small sessions, can help you regain mental clarity and emotional balance. You can practice these techniques even in a confined environment, and they can be especially helpful in maintaining peace of mind.

- Exercise and Physical Activity: Physical activity, even in a limited space, can help release built-up tension and improve mental clarity. Regular exercise can boost endorphins (the body's natural "feel-good" chemicals), which can reduce stress and help combat feelings of depression.

- Breathing Exercises: Simple deep breathing exercises can help calm the body's fight-or-flight response, lowering stress and anxiety. Practices such as box breathing (inhale for 4 seconds, hold for 4, exhale for 4, hold for 4) can help center you in moments of distress.

5. Maintain Perspective and Find Purpose

- Stay Focused on the Future: It's easy to get overwhelmed by the uncertainty of the legal process but try to remind yourself that the legal proceedings are temporary.

There will be a conclusion, and this situation, no matter how long it feels, will eventually end.

- Engage in Meaningful Activities: Incarceration can lead to a feeling of purposelessness, but there are ways to fill your time with constructive activities. Learn something new, whether it's a skill, a trade, or a subject you've always been interested in. Many incarcerated people take advantage of educational programs, religious studies, or even artistic endeavors to help them stay mentally engaged.

- Set Small, Achievable Goals: Whether it's reading a certain number of pages, learning a new word each day, or keeping a journal, setting small goals can help you maintain a sense of accomplishment and direction. This can also improve your self-esteem during a period when you may feel down or defeated.

6. Seek Legal Understanding and Control

- Be Informed About the Legal Process: Understanding the criminal justice process, what's happening in your case, and how long it may take can help reduce anxiety about the unknown. Collaborate with your attorney to ask questions and clarify the process. Having clear, factual information can provide a sense of control over your situation.

- Trust Your Legal Representation: One of the most important things to do is trust your legal team. If you have concerns or questions, be open with your lawyer about them. A strong, trustworthy lawyer can offer guidance, build a defense strategy, and provide emotional reassurance during the uncertainty.

7. Develop Emotional Resilience

- Challenge Negative Thoughts: Negative thinking can make the emotional strain of incarceration and the legal process much worse. Practice recognizing and challenging these negative thoughts. For example, if you think, "I'll never make it through this," try replacing it with, "This is hard, but I can handle it one step at a time."

- Maintain Hope and Focus on the Positive: Focus on what you can do to move forward, even in small ways. Whether it's improving your physical health, developing mental skills, or keeping a positive outlook, cultivating hope is vital to enduring challenging times.

- Engage in Positive Self-Talk: Remind yourself that you have the strength to endure and that you can get through this difficult period. Engaging in affirmations or positive self-talk can be a powerful tool for maintaining emotional well-being.

8. Practice Patience

- Understand the Process Takes Time: The legal process can be long and unpredictable, with delays, continuances, and ongoing developments. This uncertainty can be draining but learning to accept and be patient with the process is an essential skill. Focus on the present moment rather than worrying too much about the future.

- Find Strength in Waiting: While waiting for court dates or legal outcomes, use that time to build resilience by focusing on the things you can control. This will help you stay grounded and prevent you from becoming consumed by the stress of waiting.

In Summary:

Maintaining mental health and emotional resilience during incarceration and the legal process is challenging but not impossible.

Acknowledging your feelings, focusing on what you can control, seeking support, developing coping strategies for stress, and maintaining perspective are all ways to manage the emotional strain. Engaging in meaningful activities, working with your legal team, and practicing patience can help you remain focused and mentally strong as you navigate these difficult circumstances. It's important to remember that, while the situation may feel overwhelming, these strategies can provide structure, purpose, and hope throughout the process.

These methods are good to use throughout your term of incarceration, whether it's before trial or after trial. These methods helps if you get convicted and have to wait on appeals and other legal procedures to gain your liberty.

Prior to Sentencing: Information the Accused Needs to Know

Usually, it takes about 90 days to prepare the pre-sentence investigation report, so the criminal defendant has time to prepare themselves for sentencing. During this time, it would be good to reach out to individuals who can give you support, from being able to appear before the judge at the sentencing proceedings to giving a good account or recommendation about your character. This type of support can carry weight when the judge decides to pronounce a sentence. Other things that are important for the accused to know will be explained in more detail below after a more thorough review of the Pre-Sentencing investigation Report.

A **Pre-Sentencing Report (PSR)** is a detailed report prepared by a **probation officer** in the federal criminal justice system after a defendant has been convicted (usually after pleading guilty or being found guilty at trial) and before their sentencing hearing. The PSR is a crucial document that provides the court with important information about the defendant's background, criminal history, and other relevant factors to help the judge determine an appropriate sentence. The **PSR** is the same as the **PSI** mentioned earlier in this book.

Purpose of the Pre-Sentencing Report:

1. **To Provide a Comprehensive Overview of the Defendant**:

    - The PSR includes detailed information about the defendant's **personal history**, including their family, education, employment history, mental health, substance abuse history, and any other factors that could affect their behavior and future potential for rehabilitation.
    - The report also includes an analysis of the **defendant's criminal history**, detailing prior arrests, convictions, and any relevant patterns of criminal behavior. This helps the judge understand how the defendant's past conduct may influence their future behavior.

2. **To Assess the Defendant's Role in the Offense**:

    - The probation officer assesses the **defendant's involvement** in criminal activity for which they were convicted. This is an important part of the report because it provides the judge with an understanding of whether the defendant was a leader or a minor participant in the offense. It may influence the **sentence enhancement**

or reduction based on their role in the crime.

- The PSR may also discuss whether the defendant **cooperated** with authorities (e.g., through a plea agreement or by providing assistance in other investigations), which can be a factor in reducing the sentence.

3. **To Calculate the Sentencing Guidelines Range**:
   - One of the most significant aspects of the PSR is its role in calculating the **U.S. Sentencing Guidelines** range, which is a framework for determining the appropriate sentence for a federal offense. The guidelines take into account various factors, including:
     - The **severity of the offense** (based on the offense level).
     - The **defendant's criminal history**.
     - Any **aggravating or mitigating circumstances** (e.g., whether the defendant showed remorse, whether there were multiple victims, whether the defendant has a history of violence, etc.).
   - The probation officer uses this information to provide the judge with a

guideline sentencing range** (a range of months or years) for the defendant's sentence.

4. **To Assist in Rehabilitation and Sentencing Options**:

    - The PSR also provides the judge with information on whether the defendant may benefit from certain **rehabilitative programs**, such as drug treatment, mental health counseling, or educational programs. These factors can influence the judge's sentencing decision, especially if the defendant is eligible for **probation** or **early release**.

    - The report may also address whether the defendant is a **suitable candidate for supervised release** or if they are likely to re-offend. This helps the judge tailor the sentence to the defendant's rehabilitation needs.

5. **To Serve as a Check for Fairness**:

    - The Pre-Sentencing Report is important because it helps ensure fairness in the sentencing process. It provides a **neutral and objective assessment** of the defendant's background, which can prevent bias and help the judge consider all relevant factors before imposing a sentence.

- The defendant and their attorney have the opportunity to **review and object** to any inaccuracies in the report, ensuring that the sentencing decision is based on accurate and complete information.

How the Pre-Sentencing Report is Created:

1. **Investigation by a Probation Officer**:

   - After the defendant is convicted, a **probation officer** is assigned to prepare the report. This officer conducts a thorough investigation that includes interviewing the defendant, reviewing their criminal history, speaking with the defendant's family or others who know them well, and gathering any other relevant information.
   - The probation officer will also review the **defendant's financial situation**, the nature of the offense, any impact on victims, and any statements or letters of support or victim impact statements.

2. **Contents of the Pre-Sentencing Report**:

   - **Personal Information**: Includes the defendant's age, education, employment history, family background, and substance abuse history.

- **Criminal History**: A detailed account of the defendant's prior criminal offenses, arrests, and convictions.
- **Offense Conduct**: A summary of the crime for which the defendant has been convicted, including the defendant's role in the offense.
- **Sentencing Guidelines Calculation**: The probation officer calculates the sentencing guidelines range based on the nature of the offense and the defendant's criminal history.
- **Victim Impact**: If applicable, statements about the impact of the crime on the victim(s) may be included.
- **Defendant's Sentencing Request**: Sometimes, the defendant's defense attorney will submit a statement outlining their arguments for a lesser sentence (e.g., due to mitigating factors like cooperation with authorities, remorse, or personal circumstances).

3. **Review and Disclosure**: Once the PSR is completed, the defendant and their attorney have the right to **review** the report. If they believe any information is inaccurate, they can object to specific findings.

- The probation officer may revise the report based on these objections, but if the parties do not agree on the content, they can present their objections to the judge for a resolution.

Why the Pre-Sentencing Report is Used in a Federal Criminal Proceeding:

1. **Guiding Sentencing Decisions**: The most important reason for the PSR is to provide the judge with a **comprehensive, objective assessment** of the defendant's background and involvement in the crime. This helps ensure that the sentence is **fair**, consistent, and tailored to the individual defendant's circumstances.
2. **Ensuring Compliance with Sentencing Guidelines**: The federal sentencing guidelines are designed to promote consistency and fairness across the criminal justice system. The PSR helps the judge apply these guidelines appropriately by calculating the recommended sentencing range, taking into account the seriousness of the offense and the defendant's criminal history.
3. **Balancing Aggravating and Mitigating Factors**: The PSR allows the judge to weigh **aggravating factors** (e.g., the defendant's

prior criminal history or the severity of the crime) against **mitigating factors** (e.g., the defendant's cooperation with authorities or demonstrated remorse). This ensures that the sentence reflects not only the crime itself but also the defendant's potential for rehabilitation and their character.

4. **Providing Insight into Rehabilitation and Supervision Needs**: The PSR can provide valuable information on the defendant's **mental health**, **substance abuse**, and **educational needs**, which can help the judge determine whether alternative sentences like **probation**, **community service**, or **rehabilitative programs** are appropriate.
5. **Transparency and Fairness**: By providing the defendant and their attorney with a chance to review the report and object to inaccuracies, the PSR helps ensure that the sentencing process is transparent and fair. This promotes the defendant's right to a fair trial and ensures that decisions are based on accurate, complete information.

A **Pre-Sentencing Report (PSR)** is a key document in the federal criminal sentencing process. It is prepared by a probation officer and provides the judge with a thorough understanding of the defendant's background, criminal history, and the nature of the offense. The report is used to help calculate the **appropriate sentence** based on the **U.S. Sentencing Guidelines**, ensuring that the sentence is fair, consistent, and individualized. The PSR also allows for consideration of the defendant's potential for rehabilitation and helps guide decisions about programs or alternatives to incarceration. Overall, the PSR is vital to ensure that sentences are just, based on accurate information, and tailored to the defendant's specific circumstances.

During any sentence proceedings is when the criminal defendants are allowed to make their own allocutions. Under federal law a criminal defendant has the right to allocution. See below:

The Importance of Preparing and Presenting an Allocution in Sentencing

In the context of a **criminal sentencing hearing**, an **allocution** is a formal statement made by a defendant before the judge imposes a sentence. This is typically a moment when the defendant can speak directly to the court to express remorse, explain their actions, provide context for their behavior, and ask for leniency. Preparing and presenting a well-thought-out allocution is crucial for several reasons, both for the defendant's immediate case and for the broader context of their rehabilitation and future.

Here are key reasons why it's important for a criminal defendant to prepare and present an allocution during sentencing:

1. Personal Responsibility and Remorse:

- **Why It's Important**: By speaking directly to the court, the defendant has an opportunity to express **remorse** for their actions and show that they take responsibility for their behavior. A sincere and heartfelt allocution can demonstrate to the judge that the defendant is aware of the harm caused by their actions and is taking steps to make amends.
- **Impact on Sentencing**: Courts often consider a defendant's **remorse** and acceptance of responsibility when determining the sentence. A defendant who shows genuine contrition may receive a more lenient sentence than one who fails to acknowledge the harm they caused or who remains unrepentant. The **Federal Sentencing Guidelines** allow for a **reduction** in the sentence if the defendant accepts responsibility for their conduct (usually a 2-level reduction).

2. Humanizing the Defendant:

- **Why It's Important**: A defendant is often viewed through the lens of the crime they've committed, but an allocution allows the court to see the **person behind the crime**. This is particularly important in cases where the defendant may be a first-time offender or someone who committed the offense due to **circumstances** such as financial hardship, addiction, or mental illness.

- **Impact on Sentencing**: An effective allocution can help the judge understand the **nuances** of the case, such as factors that may have contributed to the crime or how the defendant has since **changed**. For example, if a defendant mentions seeking therapy or attending rehabilitation, it can demonstrate their commitment to reform and make the court more inclined to impose a sentence that is conducive to rehabilitation rather than just punishment.

3. **Building Trust and Credibility:**

- **Why It's Important**: Speaking at the sentencing hearing is an opportunity to establish the defendant's **credibility** in the eyes of the court. A defendant who respectfully addresses the court and offers a sincere, well-prepared statement can build trust with the judge. This can play a significant role in how the judge views the defendant's potential for **rehabilitation** and **future behavior**.

- **Impact on Sentencing**: Courts appreciate defendants who show **maturity**, **respect for the legal process**, and a willingness to be accountable for their actions. It's important for the defendant to be honest and not try to shift blame or minimize their crime during allocution. Being truthful and transparent can help the defendant come across as credible and deserving of a chance at **reform**.

4. Opportunity to Provide Context and Mitigating Factors:

- **Why It's Important**: Allocution provides an opportunity for the defendant to offer **mitigating factors** that the court might not otherwise be aware of. For example, the defendant may discuss how the crime occurred in the context of a personal struggle or show how they have since **changed their life** in a positive direction.
- **Impact on Sentencing**: Judges are often tasked with weighing **aggravating** and **mitigating** factors when deciding on a sentence. A defendant's statement can help introduce additional factors that might lessen the severity of the sentence. For example, if the defendant is a parent of young children or has a history of mental health issues, these factors might influence the judge to impose a more lenient

sentence or to consider alternatives to incarceration, like **probation** or **community service**.

5. Emotional Appeal and Support from Loved Ones:

- **Why It's Important**: In addition to the defendant's own allocution, having **family members** or **friends** speak on their behalf during sentencing can have a powerful impact. Loved ones can provide **context** about the defendant's character, support system, and the **positive steps** they have taken since the crime. They may speak to the defendant's **history of good behavior**, personal struggles, or their commitment to making amends.
- **Impact on Sentencing**: Letters from loved ones, or even live testimony, can help the judge view the defendant as a human being who is supported by a community and is **more than just the crime** they committed. This can also demonstrate that the defendant has a support system in place to help them reintegrate into society successfully, reducing the risk of reoffending. Judges may be more inclined to impose sentences that involve **rehabilitative efforts** (e.g., drug treatment, counseling, or educational programs) rather than punitive ones if they see that

the defendant has emotional and practical support.

6. **Demonstrating Commitment to Change:**

- **Why It's Important**: Allocution is a chance for the defendant to show the court that they are committed to **changing** their behavior. If the defendant has already taken steps toward self-improvement, such as enrolling in rehabilitation programs, working with a counselor, or volunteering, this can be mentioned as part of the allocution.
- **Impact on Sentencing**: A defendant who actively demonstrates an effort to reform may be seen as **less of a risk** for reoffending and more likely to benefit from **rehabilitative programs**. The judge may take this into account when deciding whether to impose a **long prison sentence** or provide a sentence more focused on rehabilitation, such as **probation** or **community service**.

7. **Encouraging Judicial Mercy and Leniency**:

- **Why It's Important**: An allocution is also an opportunity for the defendant to make a **personal appeal** to the judge for mercy. This is not about avoiding responsibility but asking for a sentence that reflects the defendant's potential for change. The defendant can express that they understand the harm they've caused and that they are ready to make amends.

- **Impact on Sentencing**: Many judges take into account the personal appeal for leniency, especially when the defendant shows **genuine remorse** and explains why a lesser sentence would be more appropriate given the circumstances. This can be particularly important if the defendant has no criminal history, is young, or is dealing with underlying issues such as addiction.

For these reasons, the allocution process is a key part of a defendant's sentencing and can play a crucial role in determining the final outcome of their case.

During the Sentencing you will learn or hear a lot about the federal sentencing guidelines and this manual will consist of chapters which are provisions inside the book that guide the court, probation department and the prosecutor to find a sentence.

Sentencing

After the pronouncement of the sentencing if the defendant had not waived their appeal (in a plea agreement or in open court), then it would be a good time for the defendant to consider filing a direct appeal, those who haven't wave that right they will be given notice by the judge that they have 14 days to file a notice of appeal. If the attorney that is representing the defender do not file a notice of appeal within 14 days of the pronounce of the sentencing that appeal has been exhausted as far as that right goes which means that you do not get to file an appeal because the 14 days has expired. It would be good to state for the record that you wish to file an appeal. This will put the lawyer on the spot so they will have to act accordingly to your request.

Valid Information:

Anything you say in open court is recorded because the whole court proceedings are recorded and transcribed by a court reporter who is known professionally as a stenographer.

The definition of stenographer is a person whose job it is to transcribe speech in shorthand usually for court proceedings.

In a federal court sentencing, if the defendant faces potential enhancements that could increase the severity of their sentence, there are several things they can do to address the situation and potentially mitigate the impact of these enhancements:

1. **Review the Presentence Investigation Report (PSR):** The defendant and their attorney should carefully review the PSR,

which is prepared by the probation office. The PSR includes information about the offense, the defendant's criminal history, and any potential sentencing enhancements. If there are inaccuracies in the report or factual errors, these should be addressed before sentencing.

2. **Challenge the Enhancements (If Applicable):** If the enhancements are based on facts that the defendant disputes (e.g., prior convictions, role in the offense, or aggravating circumstances), they may challenge those facts at the sentencing hearing. The defendant has the right to object to any enhancements that they believe are not supported by sufficient evidence or are incorrect.

3. **Present Mitigating Evidence:** Even if the enhancements apply, the defendant may present mitigating factors to counteract the effect of the enhancements. These could include:

   - **Personal History and Circumstances:** Showing the defendant's background, such as family support, employment history, or rehabilitation efforts.
   - **Remorse and Acceptance of Responsibility:** Demonstrating that the defendant has accepted responsibility

for their actions and shown genuine remorse.

- **Positive Contributions to Society:** Providing evidence of the defendant's positive efforts after the offense, such as participation in educational programs, community service, or counseling.

4. **Negotiate a Plea Agreement:** If not already in place, a defendant may negotiate a plea agreement with the government that addresses sentencing issues, including potential enhancements. A plea agreement can sometimes allow the defendant to agree to specific terms in exchange for a reduced sentence or the removal of certain enhancements.

5. **Prepare for a Sentencing Memorandum:** The defense attorney may submit a sentencing memorandum to the court, outlining arguments for a lower sentence or requesting a variance from the sentencing guidelines. This document may present legal arguments, factual disputes, and mitigating circumstances that could persuade the judge to impose a sentence at the lower end of the guidelines or avoid certain enhancements.

6. **Consult with an Experienced Sentencing Expert:** Defendants may consider working with a sentencing expert, such as a

forensic psychologist or a sentencing mitigation specialist, who can provide expert testimony or documentation about the defendant's mental health, background, or other factors that might mitigate the sentence.

Ultimately, the goal is to ensure that the defendant's sentence is as fair and just as possible, given the circumstances of the case and any applicable sentencing enhancements. An experienced defense attorney will play a key role in navigating this process and advocating for the defendant's interests at sentencing.

After Sentencing information

Just because you've gotten sentenced doesn't mean that the fight is over because now you have a chance to mitigate the term of imprisonment you received in the court whether you pled guilty or not and whether you waived your rights to pursue collateral relief. This is why.

Most defendants that catch a federal case have prior convictions and every sentence is based upon the prior convictions, which is the center building block for building a sentence against most federal defendants. (If you are a first-time offender, this does not apply to you because you had no prior convictions.)

When you receive your sentence and if the court uses your prior convictions to sentence you, you can go back through the state where you caught your case and file a post-conviction motion for ineffective assistance of counsel if you had an attorney. **See** the cases below.

The process I'm referring to involves the ability of a criminal defendant to challenge a **federal sentence** based on the **vacation** or **expungement** of a **prior state conviction** used to enhance that sentence.

This type of **collateral attack** allows a defendant to seek relief if the prior conviction, which was used to enhance their federal sentence, is later found to be invalid or vacated by a state court. This right is outlined in several cases, such as **Sherodney Steward (2011)**, **Custis v. United States (1994)**, **Daniels v. United States (2005)**, and **Johnson v. United States (2015)**. Let's break down this process using these key cases.

Overview of the Process:

1. **Collateral Attack on a Federal Sentence:**
    - When a defendant is convicted in federal court, their **criminal history** is often used to enhance the sentence, particularly if prior convictions are involved. These prior convictions may be state-level convictions.
    - However, if the defendant can show that one of these prior state convictions is invalid (e.g., it was vacated, overturned, or expunged), this may provide grounds for a **collateral attack** on the **federal sentence**. This means the defendant can argue that their federal sentence should be reduced or reconsidered because the enhanced sentence was based on a flawed prior conviction.

2. **State Court Vacatur or Expungement:**

- If a defendant challenges a prior state conviction and succeeds in having it **vacated** (invalidated) or **expunged**, the **federal court** may need to reassess the defendant's sentence, since the prior conviction used to enhance the sentence no longer stands.
- The defendant's eligibility for collateral relief can hinge on whether the state court vacated the conviction before the federal case was final.

Key Case Law Analysis:

1. **Sherodney Steward v. United States (2011, 11th Circuit):**
    - The **11th Circuit** held that a **defendant could challenge the validity of prior state convictions** used to enhance a federal sentence, even if those convictions were not directly challenged during the federal case.
    - The **court reasoned that when a defendant timely attacks a state conviction**, such as through a motion for vacatur in state court, that could provide grounds for a **collateral attack** in the federal system. This is important because, once a prior conviction is vacated or set aside in state court, it **cannot be used to enhance a federal**

sentence. If the prior conviction was used to enhance the guidelines sentencing range or the Statutory minimum or maximum It must be subtracted from either one to lower the initial sentence.

- **Application**: If a defendant's state conviction is vacated or expunged, and that conviction was used as a sentencing enhancement in federal court, the defendant could challenge their federal sentence and potentially have it reduced or modified.

2. **Custis v. United States (1994, U.S. Supreme Court):**

   - In **Custis**, the U.S. Supreme Court ruled that a federal defendant cannot challenge the validity of a prior state conviction used for sentencing enhancement unless the defendant can show that the conviction was **unconstitutionally obtained** (e.g., without counsel if the right to counsel was violated).

   - **Custis** limited the scope of **collateral attacks** by holding that, unless the prior conviction was unconstitutional, a defendant cannot use a **federal case** to challenge it. However, if a **state court vacates or expunges** the conviction, this would remove the grounds for the enhancement, and the defendant can seek a **re-sentencing** in federal court.

- **Significance**: While **Custis** makes it harder for defendants to challenge prior convictions in federal court, it allows for challenges if the state conviction is later vacated, as those convictions cannot serve as a basis for sentencing enhancements.

3. **Daniels v. United States (2005, U.S. Supreme Court):**

   - In **Daniels**, the Supreme Court addressed the issue of whether a defendant's prior convictions could be used to enhance a federal sentence if they were later challenged as invalid.
   - The Court held that a defendant cannot collaterally attack prior state convictions during a federal sentence proceeding unless the defendant is **challenging the conviction for constitutional defects**.
   - However, just like in **Custis**, if the prior conviction is **vacated** or **set aside** by a state court, it cannot be used to enhance a federal sentence.

- **Significance**: This ruling reinforces the idea that prior state convictions used to enhance a federal sentence must be valid at the time of sentencing. If vacated, the federal sentence should be reconsidered.

4. **Johnson v. United States (2015, U.S. Supreme Court):**

- In **Johnson**, the U.S. Supreme Court ruled that certain provisions of the **Armed Career Criminal Act (ACCA)** were unconstitutionally vague, and as a result, defendants sentenced under those provisions could have their sentences **vacated**.
- Specifically, the Court held that a **prior conviction** used to enhance a sentence under ACCA could be **vacated**, and the defendant could be **resentenced** based on the remaining valid convictions.

  - **Application**: This decision confirmed that **federal courts** must **reassess sentences** when prior convictions used to enhance the sentence are later found to be unconstitutional or invalid. If a state court vacates a prior conviction, it may trigger a **resentencing** in federal court.

Procedures used to Collateral Attack Federal Sentence

1. **Defendant Challenges Prior State Conviction:**

   A defendant may file a motion in **state court** to vacate or expunge a prior conviction used to enhance their federal sentence. This may involve arguing that the conviction was **unconstitutional** or that there were procedural issues (such as the denial of counsel).

2. **State Court Vacates the Conviction:**

   If the state court agrees and **vacates** the conviction, it means the conviction is no longer valid, and it cannot be used in federal sentencing enhancements.

3. **Defendant Files for Collateral Relief in Federal Court:**

   Once the state conviction is vacated, the defendant can file a **motion for post-conviction relief** (such as under **28 U.S.C. § 2255**) in federal court. This motion argues that the **federal sentence should be reconsidered** because the prior conviction that enhanced the sentence is no longer valid.

4. **Federal Court Reviews the Motion:**

The federal court will consider whether the vacated state conviction played a significant role in the defendant's federal sentence. If it did, the defendant could be entitled to **resentencing**, where the court may reduce the sentence or remove the enhancement related to the vacated conviction.

5. **Resentencing and Reduced Sentence:**

   If the federal court determines that the **vacated conviction** is no longer valid and was critical to the original sentence enhancement, the defendant may be **resentenced**. The new sentence may be lower if the enhancement based on the vacated conviction is no longer applicable.

Conclusion:

The process of challenging a federal sentence based on a vacated or expunged state conviction hinges on several key principles outlined in **Sherodney Steward**, **Custis**, **Daniels**, and **Johnson**. The general procedure allows a criminal defendant to seek **collateral relief** in federal court if a prior conviction used to enhance their sentence is **vacated** by a state court. Once the prior conviction is invalidated, the defendant may be eligible for **resentencing** in federal court, and their sentence may be reduced if the enhanced conviction is no longer valid.

Below are other cases that show that this is a valid process and tool to use after sentencing in federal court, providing a means for you to get back in court to attack the prior conviction that was used to give you a criminal history score based on the points used under the sentencing table or an enhanced sentence for a 924(e) or ACCA armed career criminal or a career criminal under USSG 4B1.1.

1. **United States v. Tatum (2006)**:

   In this case, the court held that a federal defendant may be entitled to **collateral relief** (i.e., reconsideration of their conviction or sentence) if they can show that the prior conviction used against them in federal sentencing was later vacated or overturned in state court.

2. **28 U.S.C. § 2255** (Post-Conviction Relief):

   This statute provides the procedure for a federal criminal defendant to challenge their conviction or sentence after their direct appeal has been denied or after serving time. While § 2255 applies specifically to federal convictions, defendants can argue that their sentence should be reduced if prior state convictions have been vacated.

3. **State Court Expungement**:

   While the **federal system** does not allow for **expungement** of criminal records in the same way that state courts can, some defendants may attempt to have prior state convictions expunged or set aside, especially if those convictions were unfairly relied upon in federal courts. In this case, the defendant may seek to use the vacated conviction as a way to challenge their federal sentence under **§ 2255**.

Process for Federal Resentencing

1. **Motion for Collateral Relief**:

   After a prior conviction is vacated in state court, the defendant may file a motion for **collateral relief** in federal court under **28 U.S.C. § 2255** or request resentencing.

2. **Court Reviews the Motion**:

   The court will determine if the vacated conviction significantly impacts the sentence or whether the defendant's criminal history is now altered due to the vacatur. If the prior conviction was used to enhance a federal sentence, the court will likely consider whether resentencing is warranted.

3. **Resentencing**:

> If the court finds that the defendant's sentence was enhanced based on the vacated conviction, the defendant may be entitled to resentencing without the enhancement, potentially leading to a reduced sentence.

The U.S. Supreme Court has made it clear that a **prior conviction** used to enhance a federal sentence can be **vacated** or **set aside**, and in some circumstances, this may result in **resentencing** of the defendant in federal court. Cases like **Johnson v. United States** have opened the door for defendants who had been sentenced under vague or unconstitutional legal provisions to seek relief, either through the **vacation of prior convictions** or **collateral relief motions** filed in federal court. While state courts may have some jurisdiction over **expungement** or **vacating state convictions**, the **federal court system** also plays an essential role in ensuring fair sentencing when a prior conviction is no longer valid.

If you did not have an attorney representing you on a state case where you took a plea and you were not made aware that the conviction could be used in the future against you to enhance other sentences whether they were state or federal, then that conviction should come off because your Sixth and Fourteenth Amendment rights to have counsel and due process of law have been violated.

State and federal law state that you should have an attorney anytime you face a felony or a conviction where you are subject to serve more than one year no matter what the charge may be. Even if it's a driving offense or misdemeanor, if you face prison time of a year or more under the law you have to be appointed an attorney. Basically, if you pled guilty and didn't waive your rights to an attorney, then that conviction should not have been used in the sentence calculus to give you a federal guideline sentence.

Most states have what they call post-conviction relief or collateral relief under the writ of habeas corpus or error coram nobis.

Habeas corpus is a fundamental legal principle that protects individuals from unlawful detention by requiring that a person under arrest to be brought before a judge or into a court. The purpose of a writ of habeas corpus is to ensure that a person's detention is not arbitrary, that there is sufficient cause or evidence to justify holding them in custody. It is instrumental in protecting individuals from arbitrary detention and ensuring that they have a fair opportunity to challenge the legality of their imprisonment. They typically do this in court by demanding that the authorities provide a valid reason or legal justification for their imprisonment.

Habeas corpus, a Latin term that translates to "you shall have the body," is a fundamental safeguard of individual liberty and serves as a check on the power of the state. It is explicitly mentioned in the U.S. Constitution and is a cornerstone of many legal systems around the world. The use of the writ of habeas corpus can be traced back to English common law and has a long history dating back to the 12th century.

Most state motions are built on the habeas corpus even though they have their own titles and individual statutes that regulate them. But they are still habeas corpus.

The cases below are cases that federal defendants have used to get back into court. United States versus Customs and United States versus McDaniels are two cases that explain that a criminal defendant cannot attack their state convictions or collateral attack under federal law. They have to go back to the state and use the state avenues that are available to them before they are allowed to bring these prior convictions before the federal court.

For instance, under the federal career offender provisions, an individual qualifies as a career offender if they have at least two prior felony convictions for either crimes of violence, drug trafficking offenses, or one of each. As explained in the previous chapter, if one of those convictions is later vacated or expunged, it may no longer count toward the career offender designation. However, simply having a conviction sealed or covered up by an attorney is not enough. Sealed convictions still apply. The prior offense/conviction must be legally vacated or expunged to be excluded under the federal sentencing guidelines.

If the criminal offender can go and get the state convictions vacated and expunged or at least start the appeal process before the filing deadline, then even if it takes an additional two or three years to get the convictions successfully removed, there is an opportunity to reduce their sentence drastically.

This is why: If you are successful when you go back through the state proceedings to get the prior conviction information off, you will be able to file a 2255, not for ineffective assistance council but to show that the prior convictions no longer apply to the federal sentencing calculus because you did your due diligence, meaning that you started attacking the prior convictions either before the convictions or after but before the 2255 became available or time expired. You will be able to show the court that you started attacking your prior convictions before your 2255 became available, which is either within one year of being sentenced or, if you file a direct appeal to the appellate court, after filing the 14-day notice once you file your direct appeal and that appeal has been exhausted by having been given a decision. The 2255 extends an additional year from the date of the denial of the appeal if it got denied. If it got granted 2255 would not have to be filed until the issue is resolved.

The key is to start preparing and attacking your state prior convictions right after sentencing or before, but before the direct appeal if possible.

Once you go back through the state, I advise anyone who is trying this to use a state post-conviction specialist who should be a paralegal, not an attorney who might charge seven times the amount of a paralegal because they not only represent you in court but also do the litigation leading up to the court proceedings. When you are filing collateral, it's not a court proceeding where you have to appear in court all the time.

You will only be able to appear in court if you are granted an evidentiary hearing based on your issues or you are successful in having state court vacated or setting aside the prior conviction showing the federal court they can no longer used the state case to enhance your federal sentence.

These convictions affect your criminal history category and also place you in a position where you can be careered out as either an armed career offender or a normal career offender.

They also are enhanced under 3559(e)which is a mandatory life sentence for certain convictions or the 851. The 851 enhancement is what they use to enhance the federal drug statute. If you face zero to 20 years and have one qualifying prior conviction that is zero to 20 years, it now goes up to 0 to 30.

If you have two prior convictions it stays the same zero to 30 years per the drug statute **21 U.S.C. 841(b)(1)(C)**. That statue has a mandatory minimum and maximum based on the drug amount charged in the indictment of an accused defendant. The official breakdown of these statues will be mentioned later on in this book.

<u>Focus on the Appeal</u>

Actually, this stage would come before the collateral preparation of a criminal case. The reason why I believe that the collateral stage should be shown to the accused criminal defendant is because prior convictions play a vital role in federal criminal enhancements under the United States sentencing guidelines and federal statutes. They should be attacked before sentencing, if possible, but at least right after because most likely they will be used in the sentencing calculation for criminal history points. Even if the accused does not get any relief on appeal, they have to place themselves in the position to have success in getting relief collaterally, and the most sought out way of getting to that point is being able to vacate or expunge the prior convictions. Let's move on.

When a criminal defendant is **sentenced in federal court** and they have **not waived their right to appeal**, the defendant has the right to pursue an **appeal** in the appellate court. The federal process governing appeals is governed by several key statutes, rules, and regulations. The main procedures leading up to an appeal include the filing of a notice of appeal, the preparation of the record, briefing the appellate court, and the final decision by the appellate court. Let's break down this process step-by-step, including the relevant laws and rules that apply.

Procedures Leading Up to the Appeal:

1. **Sentencing and Post-Sentencing Motions:**

   - After the defendant is sentenced in federal court, they can **file post-sentencing motions** if they wish. These motions include **motions for a new trial**, **motions to reduce sentence**, or **motions to reconsider the sentence**. These motions are governed by **Federal Rule of Criminal Procedure 35** (for correcting or reducing a sentence) or **Rule 33** (for a new trial).
   - However, if the defendant is not satisfied with the outcome of the sentencing or post-sentencing motions, they have the right to appeal.

2. **Notice of Appeal:**

   - **Federal Rule of Appellate Procedure 3** outlines the procedure for filing an appeal in a criminal case. The defendant must **file a notice of appeal** with the **district court** (the trial court) that issued the judgment.
   - The notice of appeal must be filed **within 14 days after the entry of judgment** or the order being appealed, as specified by **Fed. R. App. P. 4(b)**. This is a strict deadline, and failing to file

within this period may result in a forfeiture of the right to appeal.

- **Important point**: A **defendant may not waive their right to appeal** in the event of an illegal sentence or constitutional issues, but they can waive certain rights through plea agreements. If no waiver exists, the defendant retains the right to appeal.

3. **Preparation of the Record:**

- **Federal Rule of Appellate Procedure 10** governs the record on appeal. It requires that the appellant (defendant) file a **complete record** that includes all documents, exhibits, transcripts of the trial, and anything else relevant to the case. This record is typically prepared by the **district court clerk**, and the defendant may request preparation of the **trial transcript** if it is needed for the appeal.
- The **defendant's attorney** or the **court reporter** must ensure that the trial transcripts are prepared if they are necessary for the appeal.

4. **Filling the Appellate Briefs:**

- After the record is assembled, the defendant's legal counsel will file the

appellant's brief with the **Court of Appeals**.

- This brief outlines the defendant's arguments for why the conviction or sentence should be overturned.
- The **government** then files an **appellee's brief**, responding to the appellant's arguments and defending the conviction or sentence.
- The appellant may then file a **reply brief** if necessary, addressing the arguments made in the government's response.

5. **Oral Argument (if granted):**

   - In some cases, the appellate court may schedule an **oral argument**, where both parties (the appellant and the appellee) will have the opportunity to argue their case before a panel of appellate judges. However, oral arguments are not always granted, and many cases are decided solely on the briefs.

6. **Decision by the Appellate Court:**

   - After reviewing the briefs and the records, the appellate court will issue a **decision.** The court may affirm the conviction, reverse it, or remand the case back to the trial court for further proceedings.

- The appellate court's decision will be based on the **law** as applied to the facts of the case. The court may also review procedural issues, constitutional questions, or errors that may have affected the outcome of the trial or sentencing.

Relevant Statutes, Rules, and Regulations:

1. **18 U.S.C. § 3742 – Appeal of Sentence:**
   - This statute outlines the right to appeal a sentence in federal criminal cases. Under **18 U.S.C. § 3742(a)**, the defendant can appeal a sentence if they believe that it was imposed in violation of the law, was unreasonable, or was the result of an error in the application of sentencing guidelines.
2. **Federal Rules of Criminal Procedure (FRCrP):**
   - **Rule 32**: Governs the procedures at sentencing, including the right to challenge the sentencing procedures.
   - **Rule 33**: Addresses motions for a new trial, which a defendant can file in federal court if they believe there are sufficient grounds.

- **Rule 35**: Deals with the correction or reduction of sentences. This can be filed after the defendant's sentencing in some circumstances, like when there has been an error or if the sentence was unduly harsh.

3. **Federal Rules of Appellate Procedure:**

   - **Rule 3**: Specifies the requirements for filing a notice of appeal. This includes the time frame (14 days after judgment), as well as the necessary contents and filing procedure.
   - **Rule 4(b)**: Governs the time frame for filing a notice of appeal in a criminal case (within 14 days from the judgment or order).
   - **Rule 10**: Defines the record on appeal, which must include all trial documents and transcripts necessary for the appeal.
   - **Rule 28**: Provides the rules for filing an appellate brief, including the contents and formatting.
   - **Rule 32**: Discusses the procedure for filing the appellant's brief and the appellee's response brief.
   - **Rule 34**: Provides the procedure for oral arguments in appellate cases.

4. **18 U.S.C. § 3742 – Right to Appeal a Sentence:**

    - **18 U.S.C. § 3742(a)** gives the **defendant the right to appeal** a sentence if they believe it was imposed **incorrectly** (i.e., if the district court misapplied sentencing guidelines, if the sentence was unreasonable, or if it violated statutory law).

The Appellate Court's Jurisdiction:

The **U.S. Court of Appeals** has the authority to entertain the appeal, provided the defendant has filed the appropriate documents and met the requirements for an appeal. Under **28 U.S.C. § 1291**, the Court of Appeals has **jurisdiction** to hear appeals from final decisions of district courts. This includes criminal cases, such as those involving federal convictions and sentences.

1. **Jurisdiction of the U.S. Court of Appeals:**

    - The Court of Appeals has jurisdiction over federal criminal appeals once the defendant has exhausted their rights in the district court, and the defendant's appeal is properly filed. This is governed by **28 U.S.C. § 1291**, which grants appellate jurisdiction over final decisions of district courts.

2. **Enabling Statutes for Appeal:**

    - **18 U.S.C. § 3742**: As noted earlier, this statute specifically governs the **right to appeal** sentences in criminal cases. The appellate court can review sentences for errors in the application of the sentencing guidelines, unreasonable sentences, and other legal issues.

    - **28 U.S.C. § 1291**: This statute provides the appellate jurisdiction over all final judgments or orders from a district court. Once the defendant's case is concluded in the district court, they have the right to appeal the final decision to the appellate court.

Summary of the Appeal Process:

1. **File a notice of appeal within 14 days of judgment** (**Fed. R. App. P. 4(b)**).

2. **Prepare the record** of the trial, which includes transcripts, exhibits, and documents relevant to the case (**Fed. R. App. P. 10**).

3. **Submit appellate briefs** outlining legal arguments and why the conviction or sentence should be reversed or modified (**Fed. R. App. P. 28**).

4. The **Court of Appeals** reviews the case, including any oral arguments, and issues a

decision based on the legal principles involved (**28 U.S.C. § 1291**; **18 U.S.C. § 3742**).

5. This entire process is governed by the rules of the **Federal Rules of Appellate Procedure**, relevant **statutes**, and decisions from higher courts, which together ensure a structured, lawful method for challenging criminal convictions or sentences in the federal.

When a defendant appeals for a conviction or sentence in the **federal courts of appeals**, they raise **legal issues** that they believe could have impacted their case. The issues that can be addressed in a federal criminal appeal typically relate to **errors made during trial**, **violations of constitutional rights**, or **mistakes in sentencing**. In particular, two important issues often raised on appeal are:

1. **Errors in Sentencing (Application of Sentencing Guidelines)**
2. **Constitutional Violations (such as Ineffective Assistance of Counsel or Unlawful Search and Seizure)**

Let's discuss each of these issues in detail, with case law examples to validate these concerns.

1. Errors in Sentencing (Application of Sentencing Guidelines)

Issue: The defendant may argue that the trial court incorrectly applied the **Sentencing**

Guidelines or imposed a **sentence that was unreasonable** or disproportionate. These issues can arise from miscalculations of the offense level, improper upward or downward departures from the sentencing guidelines, or an unreasonable sentence that doesn't align with the statutory requirements.

Relevant Case Law:

1. **United States v. Booker (2005)**: In this landmark case, the U.S. Supreme Court held that the **Sentencing Guidelines** were **advisory**, rather than mandatory, and that courts must consider them, but can deviate from them if a sentence is "reasonable" in light of the facts and circumstances. This decision fundamentally changed how appellate courts evaluate sentences.

   Key Takeaway: If a sentence is challenged on appeal due to an error in applying the sentencing guidelines, the appellate court must consider whether the sentence is "reasonable" under **Booker**, even if it deviates from the guidelines.

2. **Gall v. United States (2007)**: In **Gall**, the Supreme Court reiterated the standard for reviewing sentences for reasonableness, emphasizing that appellate courts should give **"due deference"** to the district court's judgment. An appellate court can reverse a

sentence only if the sentence is unreasonable given the facts and the guidelines.

Key Takeaway: A sentencing error raised on appeal would be evaluated for its reasonableness, with particular attention paid to whether the district court appropriately exercised discretion under **Gall**.

Application to Appeal: A criminal defendant may argue that the sentencing judge improperly calculated the offense level or that the judge imposed a sentence that was outside the range prescribed by the sentencing guidelines without sufficient justification. The appellate court will review the **reasonableness** of the sentence, considering both the guidelines and the factors laid out in **18 U.S.C. § 3553(a)**.

2. Constitutional Violations (e.g., Ineffective Assistance of Counsel or Unlawful Search and Seizure)

Issue: The defendant may argue that their **constitutional rights** were violated during the trial, such as a claim of **ineffective assistance of counsel** or a **violation of the Fourth Amendment** (unlawful search and seizure).

Relevant Case Law:

1. **Strickland v. Washington (1984)**: In this seminal case, the U.S. Supreme Court established the standard for **ineffective assistance of counsel**

claims. The Court held that to prove ineffective assistance, the defendant must show that (1) counsel's performance was deficient, and (2) the deficient performance prejudiced the defendant's case.

Key Takeaway: A defendant claiming ineffective assistance of counsel on appeal must show that their attorney's performance was not only below an objective standard of reasonableness but that this deficiency resulted in harm to the defense.

2. **Mapp v. Ohio (1961)**: This case established an **exclusionary rule**, which mandates that evidence obtained through an unlawful search or seizure cannot be used in court. If the defendant's constitutional rights were violated by a **search without probable cause** or a **warrant**, this may be grounds for appeal, especially if the illegally obtained evidence played a key role in the conviction.

   Key Takeaway: If a constitutional violation (such as an unlawful search) occurred, the defendant can appeal and seek the suppression of evidence, or the reversal of a conviction based on the violation of their rights under the **Fourth Amendment**.

Application to Appeal: In this context, a criminal defendant may argue that their counsel was ineffective because they failed to object to improper evidence or failed to present crucial defense evidence. Alternatively, the defendant may argue that evidence used against them was obtained unlawfully, violating their **Fourth Amendment rights**, and should not have been admitted at trial.

Appealing the Appellate Court's Decision (Petitioner's Right to Further Appeal)

After the **appeal** has been heard and decided by the **Court of Appeals**, the defendant, now known as the **petitioner** (if they are the party appealing), has several options, including the possibility of further review by the U.S. Supreme Court. Here's how the process works after the appellate court decision:

1. **Exhausting the Appeal Process:**

    - If the appellate court **affirms** the defendant's conviction or sentence, and the defendant wishes to **challenge the appellate court's decision**, they may seek **further review** by the **U.S. Supreme Court**.

    - However, **federal appellate decisions are generally final** unless the Supreme Court agrees to take the case. The petitioner must exhaust all appellate options before seeking a writ of certiorari (which is the process of asking the Supreme Court to review the case).

2. **Requesting Reconsideration by the Appellate Court (Petition for Rehearing):**

    - If the petitioner is dissatisfied with the decision of the **Court of Appeals**, they may **request reconsideration** by that same court. This can be done by filing a **petition for rehearing** under **Federal Rule of Appellate Procedure 40**.
    - **Rule 40** allows a party to request that the appellate court review its decision. A petition for rehearing must be filed within **14 days after the entry of judgment** unless the court specifies otherwise.
    - In the petition for rehearing, the petitioner can argue that the appellate court overlooked important facts, misapplied the law, or made some other error in its decision.

Pursuing a Writ of Certiorari to the U.S. Supreme Court:

1. **Writ of Certiorari:**

   - After the appellate court's decision is final, the defendant can seek review from the **U.S. Supreme Court** by filing a **petition for a writ of certiorari** under **28 U.S.C. § 1254**.
   - A **writ of certiorari** is a request for the Supreme Court to review the case. The Court has discretion over whether to grant or deny the writ, and it typically grants only a small number of petitions. The Court will usually take a case if it involves **important legal principles** or resolves **conflicting decisions** among the lower courts.
   - **Case Law**: The Court's decision to grant certiorari is often based on the **importance of the legal issue** or if the case has broader constitutional implications. For example, in **Roper v. Simmons (2005)**, the Supreme Court granted certiorari to review the constitutionality of executing juveniles.

2. **Procedure for Certiorari Petition:**

   - The petitioner must file the petition for certiorari within **90 days after the appellate court's judgment** becomes final. This deadline is crucial, and failure to meet it will result in the denial of the opportunity to seek Supreme Court review.

- The petition should include **reasons why the Court should hear the case**, focusing on the **legal significance** of the issues involved.
- The Supreme Court will review the petition, and if **four Justices agree** that the case should be heard, they will issue the writ and schedule oral argument.

In summary, when appealing a federal conviction or sentence, a petitioner can raise critical issues such as **errors in sentencing** or **constitutional violations** (e.g., ineffective assistance of counsel or unlawful search and seizure). After the appellate court issues its decision, if the petitioner disagrees with the outcome, they can seek **reconsideration** through a petition for rehearing and, ultimately, file a **petition for writ of certiorari** to the U.S. Supreme Court for further review.

Overview of the Federal Circuit Courts & Their Jurisdictions

The process of pursuing a writ to the Supreme Court is highly selective, with the Court granting certiorari only in a small percentage of cases, particularly those with significant **legal questions** or **constitutional implications.**

There are **13 federal courts of appeals** in the United States, and each of these courts has jurisdiction over specific geographic regions or **circuits.** Below is an explanation of the court system and how these courts are distributed across the United States, as well as a general description of their purpose and function.

Overview of the U.S. Court System

- The **U.S. Court of Appeals** is the appellate court that reviews decisions made by the **U.S. District Courts**, which are trial courts in the federal system.
- The **U.S. District Courts** are the courts of **original jurisdiction**, where federal cases are initially tried.

U.S. Court of Appeals by Circuit:

There are 13 courts of appeals, including **12 regional circuits** and the **Federal Circuit**. The regional courts are divided into circuits, and each circuit has appellate jurisdiction over a specific group of states. The **Federal Circuit** handles certain types of cases, such as appeals in patent law and claims against the federal government.

Here's a breakdown of the **13 courts of appeals**:

1. First Circuit

- **Jurisdiction**: Maine, New Hampshire, Massachusetts, Rhode Island, and Puerto Rico.
- **Court of Appeals**: **First Circuit Court of Appeals** in Boston, Massachusetts.

2. Second Circuit

- **Jurisdiction**: New York, Connecticut, and Vermont.
- **Court of Appeals**: **Second Circuit Court of Appeals** in New York City, New York.

3. Third Circuit

- **Jurisdiction**: Delaware, New Jersey, Pennsylvania, and the Virgin Islands.
- **Court of Appeals**: **Third Circuit Court of Appeals** in Philadelphia, Pennsylvania.

4. Fourth Circuit

- **Jurisdiction**: Maryland, Virginia, West Virginia, North Carolina, South Carolina.

- **Court of Appeals**: **Fourth Circuit Court of Appeals** in Richmond, Virginia.

5. **Fifth Circuit**
    - **Jurisdiction**: Texas, Louisiana, Mississippi.
    - **Court of Appeals**: **Fifth Circuit Court of Appeals** in New Orleans, Louisiana.
6. **Sixth Circuit**
    - **Jurisdiction**: Kentucky, Michigan, Ohio, Tennessee.
    - **Court of Appeals**: **Sixth Circuit Court of Appeals** in Cincinnati, Ohio.
7. **Seventh Circuit**
    - **Jurisdiction**: Illinois, Indiana, Wisconsin.
    - **Court of Appeals**: **Seventh Circuit Court of Appeals** in Chicago, Illinois.
8. **Eighth Circuit**
    - **Jurisdiction**: Arkansas, Iowa, Minnesota, Missouri, Nebraska, North Dakota, South Dakota.
    - **Court of Appeals**: **Eighth Circuit Court of Appeals** in St. Louis, Missouri.
9. **Ninth Circuit**

- **Jurisdiction**: Alaska, Arizona, California, Hawaii, Idaho, Montana, Nevada, Oregon, Washington, and the Pacific Islands.
- **Court of Appeals**: **Ninth Circuit Court of Appeals** in San Francisco, California.

10. **Tenth Circuit**

- **Jurisdiction**: Colorado, Kansas, New Mexico, Oklahoma, Utah, Wyoming.
- **Court of Appeals**: **Tenth Circuit Court of Appeals** in Denver, Colorado.

11. **Eleventh Circuit**

- **Jurisdiction**: Alabama, Florida, Georgia.
- **Court of Appeals**: **Eleventh Circuit Court of Appeals** in Atlanta, Georgia.

12. **D.C. Circuit**

- **Jurisdiction**: Washington, D.C. (Not a regional circuit, but a special one with jurisdiction over cases involving federal agencies and laws).
- **Court of Appeals**: **D.C. Circuit Court of Appeals** in Washington, D.C.

13. **Federal Circuit**

- **Jurisdiction**: This is a specialized court with nationwide jurisdiction over certain types of cases such as patent law, government contracts, and claims against the federal government.

- **Court of Appeals**: **Federal Circuit Court of Appeals** in Washington, D.C.

Jurisdiction of the U.S. District Courts

Each **Court of Appeals** is made up of multiple **U.S. District Courts** in its jurisdiction. For example, the **Fifth Circuit** covers district courts in Texas, Louisiana, and Mississippi. The **district courts** are the trial courts for federal cases.

- **Number of District Courts**: There are **94 U.S. District Courts** across the United States.
- These courts are **divided by geographic region**, and each district is responsible for handling cases within its geographic area.
- District courts have original jurisdiction over most cases, including federal criminal cases, civil cases, and some specialized cases such as bankruptcy.

Purpose of the U.S. Court of Appeals and District Courts:

U.S. Court of Appeals:

- **Purpose**: The Court of Appeals reviews cases decided in the District Courts. It primarily handles appeals related to **legal errors** made by the trial courts, such as improper instructions to juries or incorrect application of the law. It does not retry the case but examines whether the law was applied properly and whether the defendant's rights were upheld.

- **Purpose**: The Courts of Appeals are important because they serve as an **intermediate appellate body**. They are the last line of appeal for most federal cases before a case can be sent to the U.S. Supreme Court.

U.S. District Courts:

- **Purpose**: These courts have original jurisdiction, meaning they are the first court to hear cases. They conduct trials, hear evidence, and make determinations on both fact and law. Most cases in the federal system are handled in the District Courts before any appeals are made to the Court of Appeals.

The Purpose of These Courts' Existence:

1. **Checks and Balances**: The federal courts serve as a check on the power of the executive and legislative branches, ensuring that laws and actions are consistent with the Constitution.
2. **Uniformity in the Law**: The Courts of Appeals help create consistency in the

application of federal law across the country by ensuring that the same rules are applied in similar cases in different jurisdictions.

3. **Access to Justice**: These courts ensure that individuals have access to a fair process by providing opportunities for appealing judicial decisions made in the trial courts.

Map of Federal Courts and Circuits

On the next page is a basic representation of how the U.S. is divided into judicial circuits and how the Courts of Appeals correspond to the states with

The **federal appellate system** includes **13 courts of appeals** and is divided into **12 regional circuits** and the **Federal Circuit**. These courts serve an essential role in ensuring that the law is applied consistently and that federal decisions are fair and just. After cases are decided in the **U.S. District Courts**, they can be appealed to the Court of Appeals, and if necessary, further appeal can be made to the **U.S. Supreme Court**.

Each circuit and its corresponding district courts handle specific geographic areas, ensuring that justice is served across the United States in a fair and equitable manner.

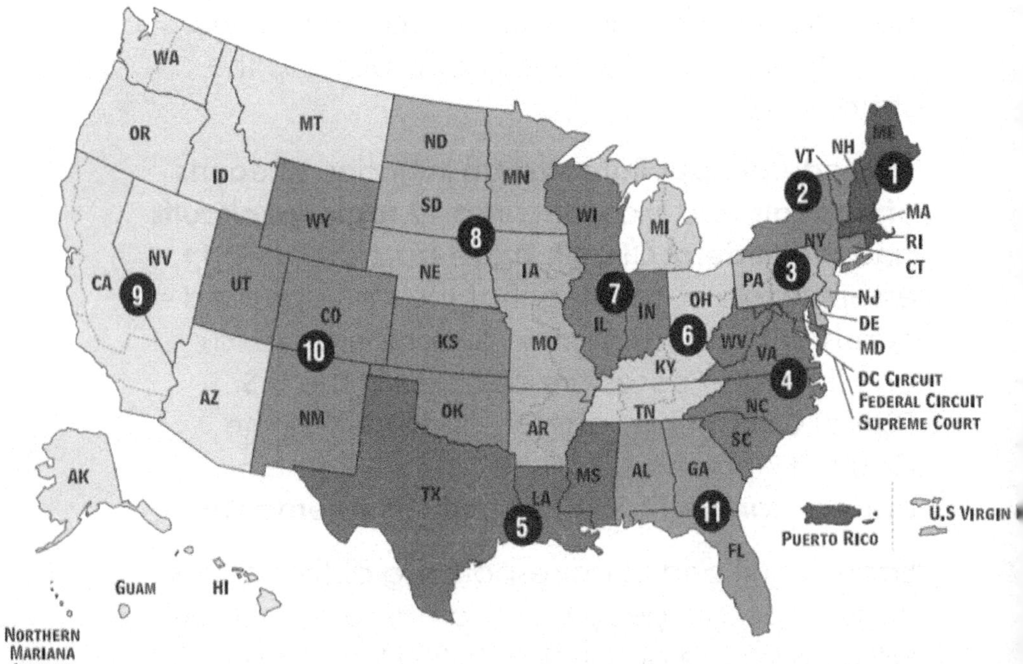

WA
OR
MT
ID
ND
SD
MN
WI
MI
WY
NE
IA
NV
CA
UT
CO
KS
MO
IL
IN
OH
KY
WV
VA
PA
NY
VT
NH
ME
MA
RI
CT
NJ
DE
MD
DC Circuit
Federal Circuit
Supreme Court
AZ
NM
OK
AR
TN
NC
SC
MS
AL
GA
TX
LA
FL
AK
HI
Guam
Northern Mariana Islands
Puerto Rico
U.S Virgin
1
2
3
4
5
6
7
8
9
10
11

<u>Writ of Certiorari</u>

This next writ is one of the very few that is actually viewed by the court because the Supreme Court has immense discretion in selecting which cases to review, granting only a small percentage of petitions it receives.

The **Writ of Certiorari** is a crucial legal mechanism in the U.S. judicial system, particularly in the context of the **U.S. Supreme Court**. It allows the Supreme Court to **selectively review** and decide whether to hear appeals from decisions made by lower federal courts (i.e., the U.S. Courts of Appeals) or state supreme courts. The process serves to ensure the consistency and uniformity of federal law, and it provides an opportunity for the Supreme Court to clarify important legal principles that may have broad implications.

Purpose of the Writ of Certiorari:

1. **Selective Review of Lower Court Decisions**: The Supreme Court has **discretionary jurisdiction**, meaning it can choose which cases to hear. The **Writ of Certiorari** is a request for the Supreme Court to review a lower court's decision. This is different from a mandatory appeal, where the court must hear the case. Through certiorari, the Court is able to select cases that involve significant **legal issues** or conflicts in the interpretation of federal law.

2. **Ensuring Uniformity in Federal Law**:
   The U.S. is a large country with many federal courts that may interpret the law differently. The **Supreme Court** ensures that there is **uniformity** in the interpretation of federal law across the country. The writ helps resolve discrepancies between lower court rulings, particularly in cases where different federal appellate circuits may have arrived at conflicting conclusions on similar legal issues. By granting certiorari, the Supreme Court can **standardize** how the law is applied across all federal courts.

3. **Addressing Constitutional Questions**:
   Another major reason the Supreme Court grants certiorari is to resolve significant **constitutional questions**. These cases may involve **fundamental constitutional issues** that could affect the rights of individuals or the relationship between the branches of government. By granting cert, the Court ensures that any important constitutional or statutory interpretation is properly addressed at the highest judicial level.

4. **Correcting Legal Errors**:
   The Supreme Court can correct **errors of law** made by lower courts, particularly when those errors could have wide-reaching effects. For example, the Court may grant certiorari to review a decision that the lower courts

misinterpreted or misapplied a federal statute or constitutional provision. The Court's decision can set binding legal precedents that lower courts must follow.

Rules Governing the Writ of Certiorari:

The rules and procedures governing the writ of certiorari are outlined in the **U.S. Supreme Court Rules**. Some of the relevant provisions include:

1. Discretionary Nature of Certiorari (Supreme Court Rule 10):

- **Rule 10** provides that the Supreme Court **has discretion** to grant or deny a petition for certiorari. The Court is not required to hear a case, and it generally chooses cases that involve important legal issues or conflicts between lower courts.
- The Supreme Court is more likely to grant certiorari in cases where:
    - There is **significant disagreement** among the lower courts.
    - The case involves **important constitutional issues** or federal questions.
    - The issue has broad **national implications**.

In short, Rule 10 gives the Supreme Court the flexibility to choose cases that have the most impact on the development of law.

2. Filing the Petition for Certiorari (Supreme Court Rule 13):

- **Rule 13** specifies the process for filing a petition for certiorari. The petition must be filed within **90 days** of the lower court's judgment, and it must follow the specific format set forth by the Court.
- The petition must include **a statement of the case**, **questions presented**, and **reasons why the Supreme Court should review the case**. The petitioner must demonstrate that the case is important enough to warrant the Court's attention.

3. The Certiorari Process (Supreme Court Rule 15):

- **Rule 15** governs the process for filing and opposing a petition for certiorari. Once the petition is filed, the **respondent** (the party opposing certiorari) has an opportunity to file a brief in opposition. After reviewing the petition and any opposition, the Justices will vote on whether to grant certiorari.
- If at least **four Justices** agree that the case should be heard, the writ is granted, and the case proceeds to briefing and oral argument.

4. Grounds for Granting Certiorari:

The Supreme Court does not grant certiorari for every case that comes before it. Some of the **main grounds for granting certiorari** include:

- **Conflict among the Circuits**: When different courts of appeals have interpreted a federal law differently, the Court may grant certiorari to resolve the conflict and ensure uniformity.
- **Important Constitutional Questions**: Cases that raise significant constitutional issues, such as challenges to federal statutes or executive actions, may be granted certiorari.
- **Federal Statutory Interpretation**: The Court may grant certiorari if a lower court has made an important ruling on the interpretation of a federal statute that could have broad implications.

Why the Supreme Court Oversees Lower Federal Court Decisions:

1. **Constitutional and Statutory Uniformity**:
   The primary reason for Supreme Court review is to maintain consistency in the application of **federal law**. Since the U.S. is divided into multiple circuits, each of which may have different interpretations of the law, the Supreme Court ensures that **federal statutes**

and **constitutional provisions** are applied uniformly across the country. Without this oversight, there could be different rules and standards in different regions, leading to confusion and inequality in the application of federal law.

2. **Final Arbiter on Legal Issues**:
   As the **highest court in the United States**, the Supreme Court is the final arbiter of **constitutional** and **federal statutory law**. By granting certiorari, the Court can issue a final, binding decision on matters of national importance, which then becomes precedent for lower courts to follow. This process provides **legal clarity** and **stability**.

3. **Resolution of Conflicts Between Courts**:
   As mentioned earlier, the lower courts (district courts and courts of appeals) sometimes disagree on how to interpret the law. The Supreme Court's role is to resolve these conflicts, ensuring that the law is applied consistently across the nation. This is particularly important for federal law, which needs to be uniform across all jurisdictions to avoid inequality.

4. **Protection of Fundamental Rights**:
   The Supreme Court also grants certiorari to hear cases that involve important **individual rights** or **constitutional protections**. For instance, cases involving the First Amendment

(freedom of speech, religion) or the Eighth Amendment (cruel and unusual punishment) may be heard to ensure that individual liberties are protected consistently across all states.

The **Writ of Certiorari** serves as the mechanism by which the **U.S. Supreme Court** exercises its **discretionary appellate jurisdiction**. It allows the Court to review decisions made by lower federal courts and state supreme courts to ensure consistency, resolve conflicts in the law, and address important legal issues. By granting certiorari, the Supreme Court ensures that federal law is applied uniformly across the country and provides final clarity on legal questions that may have significant implications for individual rights or the functioning of the federal system.

In sum, the writ is an essential tool in maintaining the integrity of the judicial system and ensuring that the **rule of law** prevails throughout the United States.

Key Terms & Definitions

Let's take a minute to go over some key terms and law that may help a lay person better understand these terms.

Ten Key Legal Terms Used in Federal Law and Their Definitions:

1. **Amicus Curiae**
   Latin for "friend of the court," this term refers to a person or organization that is not a party to a case but offers information, expertise, or insights that are relevant to the case. An amicus curiae brief can be submitted to assist the court.

2. **Certiorari**
   A writ issued by the Supreme Court to review a lower court's decision. It is a discretionary process used by the Court to decide which cases it will hear. The writ is often used to resolve conflicts between lower courts or clarify the law.

3. **Double Jeopardy**
   A legal doctrine that prevents a person from being tried twice for the same offense. The **Fifth Amendment** of the U.S. Constitution prohibits double jeopardy in criminal cases, protecting individuals from multiple prosecutions for the same alleged act.

4. **Due Process**
   A constitutional guarantee under the **Fifth** and **Fourteenth Amendments** that the government will not deprive a person of life, liberty, or property without following fair procedures. It ensures fair treatment under the law.

5. **Habeas Corpus**
   A legal action or writ by means of which detainees can seek relief from unlawful imprisonment. Under the **Habeas Corpus Act**, a prisoner can request a court to examine the legality of their detention.

6. **Indictment**
   A formal charge or accusation of a serious crime. In federal criminal cases, an indictment is typically issued by a grand jury after reviewing evidence and determining that there is enough cause to charge someone.

7. **Jurisdiction**
   The authority of a court to hear and decide a case. It refers to the geographical area or subject matter over which a court has legal power. For example, a federal court has jurisdiction over cases involving federal law or disputes between states.

8. **Precedent**

A legal principle or rule established in a previous case that is either binding or persuasive on subsequent cases with similar issues. Federal courts follow **stare decisis**, the doctrine that obligates courts to follow established precedents.

9. **Subpoena**
   A legal order requiring a person to testify as a witness or produce evidence (such as documents) in a case. Failure to comply with a subpoena can result in penalties or contempt of court charges.

10. **Tort**
    A civil wrong or injury, other than a breach of contract, that causes harm or loss to another person or entity. Federal courts may hear tort cases involving issues like negligence, defamation, or personal injury, particularly if federal law is involved.

Question: What are the two original federal laws that were around before all others and still exist today?

Answer: The two original federal laws that existed before all others and still remain in effect today are:

1. **The U.S. Constitution (1787)**

   The **U.S. Constitution** is the foundational legal document establishing the framework for the federal government. It outlines the structure of government, the powers of each branch, and the rights of citizens. The Constitution is the **supreme law of the land**, and all other laws must conform to it.

2. **The Judiciary Act of 1789**

   The **Judiciary Act of 1789** was the first statute passed by the U.S. Congress, establishing the structure and jurisdiction of the federal court system. This act created the lower federal courts and outlined the responsibilities and authority of the judicial branch, ensuring the operation of the federal judiciary.

Overlooked Strategies, Key Challenges & Post-Conviction Relief

In federal criminal trials, there are several overlooked strategies that, when employed effectively, can significantly alter the outcome of a case in favor of the criminal defendant. While common strategies such as challenging evidence, asserting constitutional rights, or using a solid defense theory are often relied upon, there are a few nuanced and less frequently used tactics that can be just as, if not more, impactful. Below are some of these strategies, along with relevant case law to provide context:

1. Impeachment of Key Prosecution Witnesses

- Strategy: One powerful but sometimes overlooked strategy is the effective impeachment of key prosecution witnesses, especially government informants or cooperating witnesses. Often, witnesses testifying for the prosecution may have credibility issues, such as prior convictions, biases, or motives to lie.
- How it can change the trial: By undermining the credibility of a key prosecution witness, the defense can cast reasonable doubt on the entire prosecution's case. This is particularly true if the prosecution's case relies heavily on

testimony from informants or individuals with significant criminal backgrounds.

- Relevant Case Law: In United States v. Abel, 469 U.S. 45 (1984), the U.S. Supreme Court held that impeaching the credibility of a witness by introducing evidence of past dishonesty or bias can be crucial to the defense. While the case involved the use of prior bad acts to impeach a witness, the principle can be applied in any case where the prosecution's key witness has a questionable history.

2. Pretrial Motions to Suppress Evidence (Fourth Amendment Violations)

- Strategy: A pretrial motion to suppress evidence obtained through an unlawful search or seizure can change the trajectory of a criminal trial. In cases involving drugs, firearms, or other contraband, the evidence obtained during an unconstitutional search is often pivotal for the prosecution.
- How it can change the trial: If the court grants the motion to suppress, it may lead to the exclusion of critical evidence, weakening the prosecution's case. Even if the motion is unsuccessful, it can serve as a point to argue constitutional violations before the jury.

- Relevant Case Law: In Mapp v. Ohio, 367 U.S. 643 (1961), the U.S. Supreme Court established the exclusionary rule, which holds that evidence obtained through unconstitutional searches and seizures is inadmissible in court.

3. Challenge to the Indictment (Fifth Amendment Violation)

- Strategy: A motion to dismiss the indictment or challenge the sufficiency of the indictment can often be overlooked. This strategy involves analyzing whether the indictment properly alleges all the elements of the crime and whether it sufficiently informs the defendant of the charges to mount an adequate defense.
- How it can change the trial: A successful challenge to the indictment may result in the case being dismissed or reduced to a less severe charge. Even a partial win on this motion can narrow the focus of the trial.
- Relevant Case Law: In Russell v. United States, 369 U.S. 749 (1962), the Supreme Court ruled that an indictment must provide sufficient detail to allow the defendant to prepare a defense, and failure to do so could be grounds for dismissal.

4. Utilizing the "Nolo Contendere" Plea Strategy

- Strategy: Although this strategy is not often used at trial itself, some defense teams may employ a "nolo contendere" (no contest) plea early in the case as part of a negotiation strategy, particularly in cases where the evidence is overwhelming. While this plea does not admit guilt, it avoids the consequences of a conviction and may allow for a more lenient sentence. (The Federal Court is very unlikely to accept a nolo plea or no contest). It's worth a try.
- How it can change the trial: In situations where conviction is likely, a well-negotiated "no contest" plea might be a beneficial alternative to going to trial. This tactic can sometimes be employed as part of plea bargaining before a trial begins, potentially securing a more favorable sentence for the defendant.
- Relevant Case Law: In North Carolina v. Alford, 400 U.S. 25 (1970), the Supreme Court held that a defendant could enter a plea of guilty (or no contest) without admitting guilt, provided the plea is made voluntarily and intelligently.

5. Jury Instructions on the Law of Accomplice Liability

- Strategy: A defense team can sometimes overlook the strategic use of specific jury instructions that clearly differentiate between the actions of an individual defendant and the role of any accomplices. This can be especially crucial in cases with multiple defendants, where the prosecution argues that all defendants acted in concert.
- How it can change the trial: Clear jury instructions on the specific elements required to prove guilt as an accomplice versus as the principal actor can result in a more favorable verdict for the defendant. Proper jury instructions can also prevent jurors from convicting based on guilt by association.
- Relevant Case Law: In Rosemond v. United States, 572 U.S. 65 (2014), the Supreme Court clarified the standards for determining accomplice liability under federal law, emphasizing that a defendant must have had knowledge of the underlying crime and taken some affirmative action in furtherance of the crime.

6. Strategic Use of the Federal Rules of Evidence (Rule 404(b))

- Strategy: Rule 404(b) of the Federal Rules of Evidence governs the admission of "other crimes, wrongs, or acts" to show things like motive, opportunity, or intent. The defense may overlook opportunities to prevent the prosecution from introducing such evidence or may fail to exploit opportunities to admit certain evidence under this rule.
- How it can change the trial: The improper admission of evidence of prior bad acts may unfairly prejudice the jury against the defendant. A defense lawyer must be vigilant in opposing the introduction of irrelevant or prejudicial prior acts and may also use Rule 404(b) to introduce evidence of the defendant's character or lack of prior bad acts to undermine the prosecution's case.
- Relevant Case Law: In Huddleston v. United States, 485 U.S. 681 (1988), the U.S. Supreme Court discussed the circumstances under which other-acts evidence can be admitted and how it must be narrowly tailored to avoid unfair prejudice.

7. Effective Use of Closing Argument

- Strategy: Sometimes overlooked, the closing argument can be a defendant's last and most impactful opportunity to persuade the jury. It's important not only to summarize the evidence but also to emphasize gaps, inconsistencies, and unanswered questions that point to reasonable doubt.
- How it can change the trial: An effective closing argument can remind jurors that the prosecution has the burden of proof and that any doubt should result in an acquittal. In cases where the evidence against the defendant is circumstantial, the closing argument can play a crucial role in emphasizing reasonable doubt.
- Relevant Case Law: The principles from Caldwell v. Mississippi, 472 U.S. 320 (1985), which emphasizes the prosecutor's duty to prove guilt beyond a reasonable doubt, can inform closing arguments, particularly when reminding jurors about the presumption of innocence.

8. Sufficiency of Evidence

Jackson v. Virginia (1979) is a landmark case in U.S. constitutional law that addresses the issue of **sufficiency of evidence** required to convict a criminal defendant. The main issue in this case was whether the evidence presented at trial was sufficient for a rational jury to find the defendant guilty beyond a reasonable doubt.

Facts of the Case:
The defendant, Jackson, was convicted of **rape** and **murder** in Virginia. At trial, the prosecution's case was based on circumstantial evidence, including the victim's identification of Jackson as her attacker and the physical evidence that was linked to him. However, Jackson appealed his conviction, arguing that the evidence presented at trial was insufficient to support the jury's verdict beyond a reasonable doubt.

Issue:
The primary issue in **Jackson v. Virginia** was whether the **due process clause of the Fourteenth Amendment** requires a court to overturn a conviction when, after viewing the evidence in the light most favorable to the prosecution, no rational jury could have found the defendant guilty beyond a reasonable doubt.

The Court's Ruling:
The **Supreme Court of the United States** ruled in favor of Jackson, establishing an

important standard in criminal law regarding the sufficiency of evidence in criminal convictions. The Court held that:

- **The Due Process Clause** (of the Fourteenth Amendment) requires that there must be sufficient evidence for any rational jury to find the defendant guilty beyond a reasonable doubt.

- **Judicial review** of the sufficiency of the evidence is not about reweighing the evidence or assessing credibility, but about ensuring that, when viewing the evidence in the light most favorable to the prosecution, there is enough evidence for any rational trier of fact (the jury) to have found the defendant guilty.

Impact: The ruling in **Jackson v. Virginia** established the **"Jackson standard"** for evaluating the sufficiency of evidence in criminal cases. This standard is applied when an appellate court reviews a criminal conviction to determine whether the evidence presented at trial was enough to support the verdict. Essentially, the Court clarified that an appellate court should not overturn a conviction unless no reasonable jury could have found the defendant guilty based on the evidence presented.

In summary, **Jackson v. Virginia** centers on the issue of whether the evidence in a criminal case was sufficient for a rational jury to convict the defendant beyond a reasonable doubt, and it set a standard for how appellate courts should evaluate the sufficiency of evidence in criminal cases.

Federal criminal defense lawyers can benefit from employing these often-overlooked strategies to increase the likelihood of a favorable outcome for the defendant. While traditional methods like challenging evidence and presenting a defense theory remain central, the use of pretrial motions, strategic impeachment of witnesses, and specific jury instructions are powerful tools in the hands of a skilled attorney. These strategies, combined with a thorough knowledge of case law and legal precedents, can significantly influence the trajectory of a criminal trial.

From this point on I will be going over collateral review and the potential motions that can aid a criminal defendant in reducing their sentence or being able to go back and get a new plea deal or a new trial based on relevant issues that are honored by the federal courts.

Collateral Review in the context of **federal postconviction relief** refers to the process by which a convicted individual challenges their conviction or sentence after their direct appeal has been denied or concluded. Unlike an appeal, which generally involves reviewing the trial record to determine if errors occurred that affected the outcome of the case, collateral review allows for challenges based on constitutional violations, new evidence, or other claims that were not or could not be raised during the direct appeal process.

Importance of Collateral Review:

1. **Preserving Constitutional Rights:** Collateral review is vital because it provides a means of ensuring that a person's constitutional rights were not violated during the trial process. For example, if a defendant's trial attorney was ineffective, if there was prosecutorial misconduct, or if new evidence surfaces that could exonerate the defendant, collateral review becomes an essential mechanism to correct potential miscarriages of justice.
2. **Postconviction Relief Options:** Federal postconviction relief is most commonly pursued through a **§ 2255 motion** (for federal cases) or a **habeas corpus petition** (for state cases). These mechanisms allow defendants to argue that their conviction

or sentence was unlawful due to issues such as:

- Ineffective assistance of counsel
- Newly discovered evidence
- Constitutional violations (e.g., violations of the Sixth Amendment right to a fair trial or the Eighth Amendment prohibition on cruel and unusual punishment)
- Prosecutorial misconduct
- False testimony or suppression of exculpatory evidence

The ability to challenge a conviction after a direct appeal has been exhausted makes collateral review an essential safeguard for justice, especially when the original trial was flawed, or new information comes to light.

Why More Cases Are Overturned on Collateral Review Than on Appeals:

1. **Limitations of Direct Appeals:**
   - **Narrow Scope of Review:** Appeals typically focus on errors made during the trial, such as the improper admission of evidence, jury instructions, or violations of procedural rules. However, an appellate court often doesn't have the authority to consider issues that

were not raised in the trial or on appeal, such as ineffective assistance of counsel or newly discovered evidence.

- **Procedural Barriers:** Some issues may not have been preserved properly at trial (e.g., not objected to in the moment) or may not have been known at the time of the original trial, making them ineligible for consideration during the direct appeal.

2. **Broader Scope of Collateral Review:**

   - **More Flexible Grounds:** Collateral review allows for broader claims of constitutional violations that were not addressed during the trial or appeal. This is one reason why more cases are overturned during collateral review. For example, if new evidence comes to light after a conviction, or if it is discovered that the defendant's trial attorney was ineffective, these issues can be raised in a collateral attack.

   - **Postconviction Developments:** Postconviction relief often becomes more successful as new legal theories or evidence emerge after the direct appeal process. For instance, new scientific evidence may prove a defendant's innocence or a legal precedent may be set that calls the original conviction into question.

3. **Ineffective Assistance of Counsel Claims:** One of the most common claims raised in collateral review is ineffective assistance of counsel. If the defendant can show that their trial attorney's performance was deficient and that this deficiency prejudiced their case (i.e., led to an unfair trial), it can lead to a conviction being overturned.

Preparing for a Collateral Review While Awaiting an Appeal:

1. **Documenting and Investigating:**
   - **Preserve Evidence:** While waiting for an appeal to be processed, it's important for defense counsel to continue investigating the case. This might include seeking out new evidence, interviewing potential witnesses who were not previously contacted, or finding experts who can challenge aspects of the original trial.
   - **Trial Records Review:** A thorough review of the trial records is essential. It's important to look for any potential errors, inconsistencies, or issues with how the trial was conducted. This review can form the basis for claims of ineffective

counsel or constitutional violations that might not have been raised during the direct appeal.

2. **Building a Case for Postconviction Relief:**

   - **Ineffective Assistance of Counsel Claims:** While waiting on an appeal, the defense can start preparing a claim based on the ineffective assistance of the defendant's trial counsel. This includes collecting evidence of how the defense attorney failed to provide adequate representation, such as failing to call critical witnesses, neglecting to investigate crucial evidence, or offering an insufficient defense.

   - **Newly Discovered Evidence:** If new evidence emerges that could exonerate the defendant or substantially weaken the prosecution's case, preparing to raise this evidence in a collateral review petition is critical. For instance, new DNA evidence could undermine the conviction, and it should be carefully documented and analyzed.

3. **Collaborating with Postconviction Specialists:** Some defense attorneys specialize in postconviction relief and

habeas corpus petitions. They are experts in identifying issues that were not addressed the direct appeal and in developing strategies to successfully challenge convictions. Consulting with or hiring these specialists can be a key step in preparing a strong collateral review case.

4. **Filing for Postconviction Relief Early:** If a defendant has reason to believe that collateral relief is needed, they should work with their attorney to file a **§ 2255 motion** or a habeas petition as soon as the appeal is concluded, ensuring that any legal deadlines are met. Delays can complicate the process, especially if the defendant is relying on new legal developments or evidence that could be time sensitive.

Collateral review is a critical safeguard in the criminal justice system, particularly for defendants who may have been wrongfully convicted or denied a fair trial. Because it allows for broader claims than a direct appeal and is less constrained by procedural rules, more cases are overturned through postconviction relief than through direct appeals. To prepare for collateral review, it is important for the defense to continue investigating the case, gather new evidence, and consider legal avenues such as ineffective assistance of counsel claims. This preparation should begin as soon as an appeal ensures that all avenues of postconviction relief are explored and pursued.

There are several other motions that can be filed to overturn a criminal conviction or either reduce the sentence if the Accused make a timely petition to court for a new trial. The first motion that will be explained is § 2241.

28 U.S.C. § 2241: History, Redress, and Relief in Criminal Cases

History of 28 U.S.C. § 2241:

28 U.S.C. § 2241 is a statute within the United States Code that provides a mechanism for federal prisoners to seek relief from unlawful detention. More specifically, it allows individuals who are in federal custody to file a petition for a writ of habeas corpus to challenge the legality of their detention. This statute is rooted in the ancient writ of habeas corpus, which has been a fundamental legal tool for protecting personal freedom since the Magna Carta in 1215. The writ provides a means for individuals to challenge their imprisonment or detention and is fundamental protection in both state and federal law.

The federal habeas corpus statute, **28 U.S.C. § 2241**, was enacted as part of the **Judiciary Act of 1789**, though it has been revised and updated over the years. While **§ 2241** is commonly associated with federal prisoners, it can also be applied to detainees in the military, immigration detainees, and other circumstances where an individual's liberty is constrained.

The writ of habeas corpus under **§ 2241** serves as an avenue to challenge "unlawful" detention, including cases where a defendant claims they were convicted or sentenced unjustly due to errors, constitutional violations, or other fundamental flaws in the judicial process.

28 U.S.C. § 2241 and Innocence Claims:

To address how a criminal defendant might use **28 U.S.C. § 2241** to have their case overturned, let's focus on the procedural and substantive aspects of innocence claims.

A person in federal prison may file a **§ 2241** petition if they believe they are being held in violation of their constitutional rights or if their conviction was based on an error so egregious that it invalidates the legality of their detention. Specifically, in the context of innocence, the defendant must demonstrate that they are actually innocent, meaning they did not commit the crime for which they were convicted.

Innocence Claims and the Use of 2241: While **§ 2241** is primarily used to challenge the legality of detention, it has sometimes been used by innocent defendants who have not been able to bring their claims under the usual channels, such as **28 U.S.C. § 2255** (which is the normal avenue for post-conviction relief for federal prisoners). This is often the case if the defendant has already filed their **§ 2255** motion and has been denied, or if they are asserting a new claim of actual innocence.

For a criminal defendant to succeed in overturning their conviction under **§ 2241**, they typically must meet several requirements, including:

1. **Actual Innocence**: The defendant must demonstrate they are actually innocent of the offense. This requires more than just a claim of legal error; they must provide evidence that strongly suggests they were wrongfully convicted, such as new exonerating evidence (e.g., DNA evidence, new witness testimony, or evidence of misconduct).

2. **Federal Jurisdiction and Exhaustion**: Generally, a defendant must exhaust all other avenues of relief (such as filing a **§ 2255** motion) before they can resort to **§ 2241**. However, if the defendant is claiming actual innocence and cannot present their claim under **§ 2255** because they are unable to meet certain procedural requirements (like the statute of limitations), they may be able to proceed under **§ 2241**, especially if they are able to establish that no other remedy is available.

3. **Fundamental Unfairness**: In some cases, a defendant may argue that their conviction was the result of a fundamental miscarriage of justice, such as prosecutorial misconduct, ineffective assistance of counsel, or violation of their constitutional rights.

Case Law Supporting Relief Under § 2241:

1. **In re Dorsainvil (3rd Cir. 1999):**

   One of the most important cases related to the use of **28 U.S.C. § 2241** for claims of innocence is ***In re Dorsainvil***. In this case, the Third Circuit Court of Appeals ruled that a federal prisoner who is actually innocent may file a **§ 2241** petition if they are unable to raise that claim in a **§ 2255** motion because of procedural constraints. The defendant in *Dorsainvil* had filed a **§ 2255** motion, which was denied, but he was later able to present new evidence of his innocence. The court held that in such circumstances, **§ 2241** could provide a vehicle for challenging the conviction based on actual innocence.

2. **McQuiggin v. Perkins (2013):**

   The U.S. Supreme Court, in ***McQuiggin v. Perkins***, held that a claim of "actual innocence" could be grounds for overcoming the statute of limitations for filing a habeas petition. Though the case concerned a state prisoner under **28 U.S.C. § 2254**, the principle of allowing an exception for claims of actual innocence can also be applied to federal prisoners using **§ 2241**. This means that even if a claim is untimely under **§ 2255**, a defendant may still be able to bring a **§ 2241** petition if they have compelling evidence of their innocence.

Definition of Redress:

Redress refers to the act of providing a remedy, correction, or compensation for a wrong or injury. In the context of legal proceedings, redress typically involves the process by which a court restores a person's legal rights or compensates them for harm caused by unlawful conduct. For instance, in the context of a habeas corpus petition, redress might involve overturning a conviction or providing compensation for wrongful imprisonment.

Vital Information about 28 U.S.C. § 2241:

- **Scope**: Section 2241 is a broad provision that allows federal prisoners, military detainees, and others to challenge their detention. However, it is often used in conjunction with other post-conviction relief mechanisms, like **§ 2255**, or when there are specific circumstances that make a **§ 2255** petition unavailable or ineffective.
- **Filing a Petition**: A petition for a writ of habeas corpus under **§ 2241** must typically be filed in

the district where the prisoner is being held. It must demonstrate why detention is unlawful or unconstitutional.

- **Limitations and Challenges**: One of the major limitations of **§ 2241** is that courts generally require petitioners to exhaust other forms of relief before filing a **§ 2241** petition. Additionally, it may be difficult to get relief, as the claim must be strong, and there must be clear evidence of an injustice or error.
- **Exhaustion of Remedies**: Before filing a **§ 2241** petition, prisoners generally must exhaust administrative remedies within the prison system. In certain cases, like in the case of actual innocence, courts may bypass this requirement if it is shown that the standard legal process would be ineffective.

Conclusion:

28 U.S.C. § 2241 provides a critical avenue for challenging unlawful detention, and in cases of actual innocence, it can sometimes be the only way for a defendant to obtain relief. While this statute is typically seen as a last resort, it has been essential for prisoners who otherwise have no remedy available under **28 U.S.C. § 2255** or who face new claims of innocence or constitutional violations that were not previously raised. Understanding how to use this legal tool, along with the proper case law and definitions, is key for any criminal defendant seeking to overturn an unjust conviction.

This next motion that I'm about to explain will only reduce the sentence based on new guideline changes passed by the United States Sentencing Commission or statutory changes made by the United States Congress that affect the guideline sentence.

Relief Through 18 U.S.C. § 3582(c)(2) - Motion for Reduction of Sentence

18 U.S.C. § 3582(c)(2) allows federal courts to modify a criminal defendant's sentence after the defendant has been convicted and sentenced, but only in specific circumstances. This section primarily provides a mechanism for reducing a sentence if the defendant's sentencing range has been lowered due to a retroactive amendment to the U.S. Sentencing Guidelines. These motions are often referred to as "motions for sentence reduction," and they are used by criminal defendants seeking a reduction in their sentence based on changes in the law.

Key Elements of 18 U.S.C. § 3582(c)(2)

- **Eligibility for Reduction**: A defendant is eligible for a sentence reduction under **§ 3582(c)(2)** if the sentencing range, based on the Sentencing Guidelines, was affected by a retroactive amendment.

- **Limitation**: The reduction cannot be greater than the term of imprisonment authorized by the new sentencing range under the amended Guidelines.
- **Motion Process**: The defendant must file a motion for sentence reduction, and the court has discretion to decide whether to reduce the sentence, based on factors such as the defendant's behavior in prison, whether they have served a portion of their sentence, and the nature of the crime.

Impact of 1B1.10 and the Retroactive Amendments to Drug Sentencing Laws

The U.S. Sentencing Commission has made several changes to the Sentencing Guidelines over the years, especially concerning drug offenses, and these changes can affect a defendant's sentencing range. The key rule that governs these reductions is **U.S. Sentencing Guidelines § 1B1.10**, which provides the framework for implementing retroactive amendments that lower sentencing ranges.

Notable Amendments to Drug Sentencing and Their Effects:

1. **Amendment 750 (2011)**:

- **Impact**: This amendment lowered the sentencing guidelines for crack cocaine offenses. Before this change, individuals convicted of crack cocaine offenses were sentenced much more harshly than those convicted of powder cocaine offenses, even though both drugs are chemically similar.
- **Impact on Sentencing**: Amendment 750 reduced the base offense levels for crack cocaine offenses, leading to a reduction in the sentencing range for many offenders convicted of crack-related crimes.
- **Case Law Example**: In ***Dillon v. United States*, 560 U.S. 817 (2010)**, the Supreme Court held that a defendant was eligible for a sentence reduction under **§ 3582(c)(2)** based on Amendment 750. The Court held that a district court could use the retroactive amendment to reduce a defendant's sentence if the original sentence was based on the crack cocaine guideline.

2. **Amendment 782 (2014)**:

- **Impact**: Amendment 782, also known as the **"Drugs Minus Two"** amendment, lowered the offense levels for drug trafficking offenses under the Sentencing Guidelines by two levels. This was a broad reform that affected offenders convicted of drug trafficking involving various substances, not just crack cocaine.

- **Impact on Sentencing**: This amendment led to a decrease in the sentencing range for many individuals convicted of drug offenses, especially for those sentenced under the earlier versions of the Guidelines.

How Reductions Affect Sentencing Ranges:

When the Sentencing Commission lowers the sentencing guidelines for certain offenses, such as those related to drug trafficking, the change can lead to a reduction in a defendant's sentencing range. Under § 3582(c)(2), if the guideline reduction applies retroactively, courts are authorized to grant sentence reductions, even after the defendant has already been sentenced.

For example, **prior to Amendment 750**, an individual convicted of crack cocaine might have faced a sentence under a much higher sentencing range. With Amendment 750, that defendant's sentencing range might be significantly lower, making them eligible for a reduction under § 3582(c)(2).

Similarly, **Amendment 782** affected a wide range of drug offenses. A defendant sentenced for a drug trafficking offense could file a § 3582(c)(2) motion for a sentence reduction if their offense level was lowered by the amendment.

Case Law Supporting Sentence Reductions Under § 3582(c)(2):

Several key court cases have helped define the scope and limitations of sentence reductions under § 3582(c)(2):

1. **Dillon v. United States**, 560 U.S. 817 (2010):

   The U.S. Supreme Court held that § 3582(c)(2) applies retroactively to changes in sentencing guidelines, including those involving crack cocaine offenses. The Court further clarified that a district court has discretion to reduce a sentence, but that the reduction must be consistent with the amended guideline range.

2. **United States v. Moore**, 708 F.3d 163 (4th Cir. 2013):

   The Fourth Circuit reaffirmed that the "retroactive" application of guidelines, such as Amendment 750, should be used to reduce sentences under § 3582(c)(2) for those who were originally sentenced under a higher sentencing range.

3. **United States v. Vautier**, 144 F.3d 756 (11th Cir. 1998):

   In this case, the Eleventh Circuit addressed the issue of whether a court can consider post-sentencing conduct (such as rehabilitation) when determining whether to grant a reduction under § 3582(c)(2). While the court ruled that post-sentencing conduct does not justify a reduction on its own, it held that the court could consider it as part of the overall "safety value" for reductions.

4. **United States v. Brown**, 2020 WL 607036 (5th Cir. 2020):

   The Fifth Circuit ruled that defendants can apply for reductions based on amendments like Amendment 782, even if they have previously filed other post-conviction motions.

18 U.S.C. § 3582(c)(2) offers criminal defendants an opportunity for relief if their sentencing range has been lowered due to retroactive changes in the U.S. Sentencing Guidelines. The Sentencing Commission's amendments, such as those related to crack cocaine and the "Drugs Minus Two" policy, have had significant impacts on sentencing ranges, offering reductions in sentence for many offenders. Key case law, such as ***Dillon v. United States*** and ***United States v. Brown***, supports the availability of such relief and helps clarify the scope of sentence reductions. Through motions filed under **§ 3582(c)(2)**, individuals convicted of certain offenses may seek reductions in their sentences, benefiting from the evolving nature of sentencing laws.

This motion recently mentioned above has a sister that has basically taken the federal courts by surprise because of the amount of relief it has been given out since the passing of **First Step Act in 2018**. Below I will explain the history and why this motion is so important today to the federal criminal inmates/defendants that are trying have their sentences reduced significantly or to time serve.

The Impact of 18 U.S.C. § 3582(c)(1)(A) and the First Step Act of 2018 on Criminal Defendants

The **First Step Act of 2018** significantly impacted the relief available to federal criminal defendants, specifically with regard to **18 U.S.C. § 3582(c)(1)(A)**. This section was previously more restrictive in terms of granting sentence reductions for incarcerated individuals, but the First Step Act amended it to allow for greater flexibility and broader access to sentence reductions. This change marked a pivotal shift in how federal judges and defendants approach sentence reductions and has been used to provide relief to individuals who may have previously had no recourse.

Before the First Step Act: Limited Access to Sentence Reductions

Before the passage of the First Step Act in 2018, **18 U.S.C. § 3582(c)(1)(A)** was rarely used because it had strict conditions under which a defendant could petition for a sentence reduction. Prior to 2018, § 3582(c)(1)(A) allowed a defendant to request a sentence reduction only after **exhausting all administrative remedies** with the Bureau of Prisons (BOP) or waiting 30 days from the date the defendant requested such relief from the BOP. In most cases, the **BOP** had the sole discretion to file motions for sentence reductions on behalf of incarcerated individuals. This meant that prisoners had very limited ability to petition the court directly unless the BOP supported their motion.

The BOP's approach was conservative, often denying petitions or being slow to process them, and this left many prisoners in a position where they had no meaningful way to challenge their sentences unless the BOP itself acted on their behalf. As a result, **federal prisoners** had limited access to the courts seeking a reduction in sentence, and the ability to achieve a sentence reduction under § 3582(c)(1)(A) was largely unavailable to those outside of the BOP's favor.

The First Step Act of 2018: Expanding Relief to Federal Defendants

The **First Step Act**, signed into law on December 21, 2018, made a critical change to § 3582(c)(1)(A) by allowing **federal prisoners to file motions for sentence reductions directly in court** without needing the BOP to initiate the process. This change dramatically expanded the availability of relief, enabling defendants to have direct access to the courts and request sentence reductions based on several key factors, including but not limited to:

1. **Extraordinary and Compelling Reasons**: Defendants could now present their case for sentence reductions if they could demonstrate "extraordinary and compelling reasons" for a reduction in their sentence. These reasons could include health issues, changes in the law, or rehabilitation efforts while incarcerated.

2. **Review of 3553(a) Factors**: When considering whether to reduce a sentence, federal judges are required to review the factors outlined in **18 U.S.C. § 3553(a)**. These factors include:

   - The nature and circumstances of the offense.
   - The history and characteristics of the defendant.
   - The need for the sentence imposed to reflect the seriousness of the offense and provide just punishment.
   - The need for the sentence imposed to promote respect for the law.
   - The need for the sentence to afford adequate deterrence to criminal conduct.

- The need to protect the public from further crimes of the defendant.
- They need to provide the defendant with educational or vocational training or treatment to rehabilitate them.

Judges now have the power to use these factors to reduce sentences based on a more holistic view of the defendant's situation, including their personal rehabilitation and their behavior while incarcerated.

How the First Step Act Expanded Judicial Discretion

One of the most significant impacts of the **First Step Act** was its granting of near **unlimited powers** to federal judges to **reduce a defendant's sentence** based on their interpretation of the § 3553(a) factors and a defendant's circumstances. The law shifted the focus from a rigid, inflexible system to one that is more discretionary, allowing judges to consider not just the nature of the crime, but also the individual characteristics and conduct of the defendant while incarcerated.

This **judicial discretion** has provided federal judges with the flexibility to reduce a defendant's term of imprisonment to a degree that they feel is appropriate based on the totality of the circumstances. Importantly, this is not just a reduction of a few months or years but can involve a substantial decrease in the length of a sentence if the judge finds it justified by the § 3553(a) factors.

Impact on Criminal Defendants:

1. **Increased Access to Relief**: The First Step Act allowed many inmates who previously had no meaningful way to petition for sentence reductions to now do so directly in court. For example, defendants who have demonstrated exemplary conduct, rehabilitation, or those who have developed severe health issues that make their continued incarceration unduly harsh can now seek relief.

2. **Greater Focus on Rehabilitation**: Judges can now consider how well a defendant has rehabilitated while incarcerated. This may include participation in educational programs, drug treatment, vocational training, and mental health services. For many individuals who may have previously been locked into long sentences with little chance of release, the First Step Act opened the door for relief based on personal growth and rehabilitation.

3. **Compassionate Releases**: Many prisoners with serious health issues or those over 60 years old with long sentences have benefited from the First Step Act's provisions. Defendants suffering

from terminal illnesses, debilitating conditions, or aging inmates who no longer pose a threat to society are among those who can request sentence reductions under "extraordinary and compelling reasons."

4. **Judicial Discretion and the 3553(a) Factors:**

   The **3553(a) factors** give judges a framework through which they must evaluate whether a sentence reduction is warranted, but they have the discretion to weigh these factors as they see fit. In particular, the following considerations have led to reduced sentences under the First Step Act:

   - **Rehabilitation and Good Conduct**: Judges may reduce a sentence if they believe that the defendant has demonstrated sufficient reform and rehabilitation while incarcerated. This includes involvement in programs aimed at reducing recidivism.

   - **Health Concerns**: A defendant who is suffering from serious health problems, particularly in light of the COVID-19 pandemic, may find relief under the First Step Act if their condition worsens to a point where their continued imprisonment would be unjust or cruel.

   - **Age and Time Served**: Defendants who are elderly or have served a significant portion of their sentence may also be eligible for reductions, especially if they have shown that they no longer pose a danger to society.

- **Family and Societal Impact**: Courts may also consider the impact that a sentence reduction could have on the defendant's family and community, especially for those with significant ties to their families or who are the sole providers for their dependents.

Case Law and Examples of Impactful Decisions:

Since the First Step Act passed, several courts have granted sentence reductions that highlight the broad judicial discretion provided under § **3582(c)(1)(A).** Some notable cases include:

1. **United States v. Stephens, 2020 WL 2508674**:

   A defendant, convicted of a drug offense, was granted a sentence reduction after demonstrating that the extraordinary and compelling reasons for his release (his advanced age, health issues, and time served) weighed in favor of a reduction.

2. **United States v. McCoy, 981 F.3d 271 (4th Cir. 2020)**:

   The Fourth Circuit held that a defendant's health issues (specifically, the risk posed by COVID-19) could be a sufficient basis for granting a sentence reduction under the First Step Act. This case emphasized the importance of considering a defendant's rehabilitation and health when determining sentence reductions.

3. **United States v. Glover, 2020 WL 5819035**:

   A defendant with a long history of drug offenses was granted a sentence reduction after demonstrating significant rehabilitative efforts, including completing educational and vocational programs while incarcerated.

Conclusion:

The passage of the **First Step Act** in 2018 significantly expanded the availability of sentence reductions under **18 U.S.C. § 3582(c)(1)(A)**. Before the Act, such motions were rarely used due to the limitations of the Bureau of Prisons' control over the process. The First Step Act granted federal judges' broad discretion to reduce a defendant's sentence, allowing for more individualized and compassionate consideration based on the **3553(a) factors** and **extraordinary and compelling reasons**. This change has allowed many federal defendants to receive relief based on rehabilitation, age, health conditions, and the nature of their offenses, leading to a more nuanced and rehabilitative approach to sentencing and sentence reductions.

For real, this is the best decision that was made for federal criminal defendants since the beginning of 2255. Actually, this motion replaces 2055. Based on the amount of relief that could be granted to a criminal defendant, it's the next best thing to having clemency granted in the accused's favor.

There are other habeas and collateral motions that could be filed for the criminal defendant that I will not entertain in this book because of my experience and knowledge of these motions. They have very little impact because they have time restraints and procedural hurdles that make it almost impossible to achieve any success or relief for the criminal offender. The motions I have included give you hope and a chance.

What is Clemency?

Last but not least, the criminal defendant has a petition that's not a motion. It's actually outside of the jurisdiction of the court. But if this petition is granted, it will offer you back your freedom or a sentence reduction like the motions explained above.

Pardon and clemency are tools used to provide relief to individuals convicted of federal offenses. These mechanisms are part of the President's constitutional powers to grant mercy or forgiveness to those who have been convicted of federal crimes. Clemency can take several forms, including pardons, commutations, and reprieves, all of which have different impacts on a defendant's sentence or conviction.

Clemency refers to the act of showing mercy or leniency, typically by reducing a criminal sentence or providing a pardon for a crime. Under the U.S. Constitution, the President has the authority to grant clemency to individuals convicted of federal crimes. Clemency can take several forms:

1. **Pardon**:

    - A **pardon** is a complete forgiveness for a crime. It essentially erases the legal consequences of a conviction, restoring the individual's civil rights, such as the right to vote, hold public office, or possess firearms. A pardon does not expunge or seal the criminal record, but it removes the legal consequences associated with the conviction.

- **Effect on Inmate**: A pardon does not reduce a sentence but serves as a form of forgiveness for the crime. It may be granted for moral, rehabilitative, or humanitarian reasons, and the individual is no longer subject to the legal consequences of the conviction.

2. **Commutation**:

- A **commutation** is a reduction of a sentence. This may include reducing the length of a prison sentence, changing a death sentence to life in prison, or reducing a life sentence to a fixed-term sentence. Unlike a pardon, a commutation does not forgive the crime itself but reduces the punishment.

- **Effect on Inmate**: Commutation results in a sentence reduction, which can lead to the immediate release of the inmate if their sentence is reduced to time already served, or it could result in a shorter prison term. It does not imply innocence or guilt but merely reduces the penalty.

3. **Reprieve**:

- A **reprieve** is a temporary delay in the execution of a sentence, typically used in death penalty cases. It does not reduce the sentence but postpones the punishment.
- **Effect on Inmate**: A reprieve does not lead to permanent relief but rather provides a temporary stay of execution or sentencing.

Pardon and Clemency: An Overview of the Process and Impact on Federal Inmates

The Clemency Process

The clemency process involves several steps, often beginning with a formal petition by the inmate or their legal representatives. The process typically follows these steps:

1. **Application**:

   Individuals seeking clemency usually submit a formal petition to the **Office of the Pardon Attorney** in the U.S. Department of Justice. The application includes details of the offense, the individual's record, and reasons for seeking clemency, such as personal rehabilitation or the achievement of post-conviction reform.

2. **Review**:

   The Pardon Attorney's office reviews the application, gathering information about the petitioner's case, including the nature of the offense, the behavior of the defendant while incarcerated, the time served, and any efforts at rehabilitation. The office may also gather opinions from the judge, prosecutor, or victim involved in the case.

3. **Recommendation**:

   Based on this review, the Pardon Attorney's office makes a recommendation to the President. The President, however, has the ultimate authority to grant or deny clemency. The Pardon Attorney's recommendation is influential but not binding.

4. **Presidential Decision**:

   The President can grant or deny the clemency request. If the request is granted, the President will issue a formal pardon or commutation. If the request is denied, there is typically no further recourse.

Clemency and Immediate Release

For inmates serving time in federal prison, **commutation** is the most likely path to **immediate release**. When the President commutes a sentence, the inmate's sentence is reduced, and if the new sentence matches or is shorter than the time they have already served, the individual is released immediately. Pardons, on the other hand, do not typically result in immediate release, as they do not alter the sentence but instead provide forgiveness for the crime.

Clemency Under Recent U.S. Presidents

Each U.S. president has used clemency in different ways, with varying degrees of frequency and focus. Let's look at clemency under the last three presidents:

President Barack Obama (2009–2017)

- **Clemency Initiatives**: Obama's administration was notable for its robust use of clemency, especially **commutations** for individuals serving long sentences for nonviolent drug offenses.
- **Pardon Statistics**:
  - Obama granted **1,927 commutations** during his presidency, more than any other president in U.S. history.
  - He also granted **212 pardons.**
  - His focus was largely on individuals who had been sentenced under harsh sentencing laws, particularly the **Fair Sentencing Act of 2010**, which reduced the disparity between crack and powder cocaine sentencing.
- **Notable Clemency Grants**: One of the most high-profile acts of clemency during Obama's presidency was the commutation of **Chelsea**

Manning, a former U.S. Army intelligence analyst who had been convicted of espionage-related offenses.

President Donald Trump (2017–2021)

- **Clemency Initiatives**: Trump's approach to clemency focused on several high-profile cases, often granting pardons and commutations to individuals with strong political or celebrity connections, or those with high-profile criminal cases.
- **Pardon Statistics**:
  - Trump granted **237 pardons** and **1,462 commutations**.
  - His clemency efforts included controversial actions such as pardoning individuals like **Michael Flynn**, his former National Security Advisor, who had pleaded guilty to lying to federal investigators, and **Roger Stone**, his political ally, convicted of obstruction and witness tampering.
  - Trump also granted clemency to individuals convicted of drug offenses, particularly toward the end of his presidency, including **Alice Johnson**, a criminal justice reform advocate, who had been serving a life sentence for a nonviolent drug offense.

President Joe Biden (2021–Present)

- **Clemency Initiatives**: Biden's approach to clemency has been more restrained so far, though his administration has emphasized criminal justice reform and tackling systemic issues, including racial disparities in sentencing.
- **Pardon Statistics (as of 2023)**:
  - Biden has granted **several hundred pardons and commutations**, including actions aimed at addressing **marijuana-related convictions.** In 2022, he pardoned **over 6,000 individuals** convicted of simple possession of marijuana at the federal level.
  - Biden's clemency actions also focus on people incarcerated for offenses related to **nonviolent drug crimes** and those who have shown significant rehabilitative efforts.
- **Biden's Marijuana Pardon**: A notable initiative was his **2022 pardon** for individuals convicted of marijuana possession under federal law, which was a key part of his broader criminal justice reform efforts. This included **over 6,500 individuals** who had been convicted of simple marijuana possession offenses at the federal level.

Who Reduced the Most Sentences in History?

As of now, **President Barack Obama** holds the record for the most **commutations** and **pardons** granted in U.S. history. Obama's legacy in this area is defined by his efforts to reduce sentences for those convicted of nonviolent drug offenses, many of whom had been sentenced under outdated, harsh drug sentencing laws. His administration was marked by a proactive approach to clemency, with a focus on criminal justice reform.

Conclusion:

Pardon and clemency serve as powerful tools in the criminal justice system, offering federal inmates a chance to seek relief from their sentences. The **First Step Act** and other reform measures have made the process more accessible, but clemency remains a process that ultimately relies on presidential discretion. Over the past three administrations, we have seen significant changes in the number and nature of clemency grants, with President Obama granting the most commutations in U.S. history, President Trump focusing on a high-profile set of cases, and President Biden initiating marijuana-related pardons to address racial disparities in drug sentencing.

As the clemency process continues, we may see further shifts in the scope and impact of executive mercy, as new policies and priorities in criminal justice reform evolve.

First Step Act & Other Developments

First Step Act of 2018

This book would not be complete if it didn't include the impact of the First Step Act of 2018 that issued the power of the 3582(C)(1)(A) Motion. Here is an overview of the new laws, regulations, and USSG Amendments for 2024-25.

The **First Step Act of 2018** significantly reformed the federal criminal justice system, introducing measures aimed at reducing incarceration rates, enhancing rehabilitation opportunities, and improving prison conditions. Its impact continues to shape the experiences of federal inmates and the operations of the Bureau of Prisons (BOP).

Key Provisions and Ongoing Relief

1. **Sentencing Reforms**:
    - **Retroactive Application of the Fair Sentencing Act**: The First Step Act made the Fair Sentencing Act of 2010 retroactive, reducing the sentencing disparity between crack and powder cocaine offenses. This allowed individuals sentenced under the previous 100:1 ratio to seek resentencing under the more equitable 18:1 ratio. As of January 2024, over 4,000 individuals benefited from this change.
    - **Expansion of the "Safety Valve"**: By broadening the "safety valve" provision,

the Act enabled judges to impose sentences below mandatory minimums for certain nonviolent drug offenses, providing greater sentencing flexibility.

- **Compassionate Release**: The Act empowered federal courts to grant compassionate release motions, allowing for early release due to "extraordinary and compelling circumstances," such as severe medical conditions. This provision has led to the release of over 2,600 individuals, particularly during the COVID-19 pandemic.

2. **Prison Reforms**:

    - **Recidivism Reduction Programming**: The Act mandated the development of a risk and needs assessment system to tailor recidivism reduction programs to individual inmates, addressing their specific criminogenic needs. This system has expanded educational and vocational training opportunities, contributing to a decrease in recidivism rates among participants.

    - **Incentives for Participation**: Inmates can earn up to 54 days of good time credit for every year of their imposed sentence, promoting engagement in rehabilitative programs.

- **Second Chance Act Expansion**: The Act enhanced the Second Chance Act, encouraging partnerships with nonprofit and community-based organizations to deliver recidivism reduction programming, thereby improving reentry outcomes.

Other Developments and Proposed Legislation

- **Second Look Act**: In November 2022, a federal judge utilized the First Step Act to grant early release to an inmate serving multiple life terms, citing significant rehabilitation and evolving judicial standards. This decision has spurred discussions about implementing "Second Look" legislation, such as New York's proposed Second Look Act, which would allow state judges to reassess sentences after ten years, aiming to address unjust and excessive sentences.
- **Sentencing Reform Discussions**: The Third U.S. Circuit Court of Appeals ruled that the U.S. Sentencing Commission lacked authority to enact policies allowing judges to consider changes in law as reasons for compassionate release. This decision has ignited debates about the boundaries of judicial discretion and the need for legislative clarification.
- **USSG Amendments for 2024**: While specific details of the 2024 amendments to the United States Sentencing Guidelines (USSG) are

pending, it is anticipated that these revisions will continue the trend toward sentencing reform, potentially offering reduced sentencing ranges for certain offenses and enhancing opportunities for sentence reductions based on rehabilitation efforts. Here is where you can find information about new U.S. Sentencing Guidelines (USSG) amendments, laws affecting federal criminals, and statutory laws currently before Congress:

- www.ussc.gov/topic/amendments
- www.congress.gov/legislation

Looking Ahead

The momentum for criminal justice reform is gaining traction, with bipartisan efforts focusing on reducing mass incarceration and promoting rehabilitation. The **First Step Act** has laid a foundation for these changes, and ongoing legislative and judicial actions continue to build upon its principles. Proposed laws like the Second Look Act and potential amendments to the USSG reflect a growing recognition of the need for a more equitable and rehabilitative justice system. As reforms evolve, it is crucial for inmates, legal professionals, and advocates to stay informed about legislative developments and policy changes that may impact sentencing, incarceration conditions, and opportunities for early release. Engaging with resources provided by the BOP and other official channels can offer guidance on navigating these changes and accessing available relief mechanisms.

Recent Developments in Federal Sentencing and Clemency are under review currently.

Personal Note

As the author and an Ex Federal Defendant, I want to end this book on a personal note: After dealing with a criminal situation, whether through incarceration or being accused of a federal crime, it can feel overwhelming to rebuild one's life, reputation, and sense of purpose. However, it's important to know that change is possible, and with determination, support, and the right mindset, a person can move forward and rebuild their future. Here's how someone can do it:

1. Accept the Past, but Don't Be Defined by It

The first and most important step is to **accept the past** but **not let it define you**. It's normal to feel shame, guilt, or regret, but those feelings should not keep you stuck. Recognize that everyone makes mistakes, and people have the ability to change. The key is to learn from experience and use it as a steppingstone to move forward, not as a wall that keeps you trapped.

2. Seek Professional Help and Support

Starting afresh often requires seeking **professional help**. Here are some resources to consider:

- **Therapy/Counseling**: A therapist can help you work through emotional and mental hurdles, such as feelings of shame or anxiety. They can also assist in improving your self-esteem and helping you find healthy ways to cope with your experiences.

- **Reentry Programs**: If you were incarcerated, many cities and states have **reentry programs** designed specifically to help former prisoners adjust to life outside. These programs offer support with finding housing, employment, and even mental health services.
- **Support Groups**: Surrounding yourself with others who have gone through similar situations can help a lot. **Support groups** provide a space for people to share their stories, offer advice, and build solidarity.

3. Rebuilding Your Reputation

- **Be Honest and Transparent**: Rebuilding your reputation takes time, but one of the most important things you can do is be **honest** about your past when the situation calls for it. Being upfront about your past mistakes shows that you are taking responsibility, and it helps establish trust.
- **Make Amends When Possible**: If it's appropriate and possible, consider making amends with those you may have wronged. Apologizing and taking responsibility for your actions shows growth and maturity.

- **Focus on Positive Actions**: Over time, **your actions will speak louder than words**. Volunteering, helping others, and making responsible choices will start to shift how others view you. Actions that reflect growth and improvement help rebuild a reputation based on what you are doing now, not just what happened in the past.

4. Set Personal Goals

Once you've dealt with the immediate challenges of rebuilding your life, it's important to start focusing on **personal goals** that can give you a sense of direction and purpose. Here are some tips:

- **Start Small**: Setting **small, achievable goals** is key. You might start with something as simple as finding stable employment or improving your health. Small victories can build momentum and give you the confidence to pursue bigger goals.
- **Pursuing Education**: If possible, consider furthering your education. This can be through formal schooling, online courses, or trade programs. Learning new skills opens up job opportunities and helps you feel more empowered.
- **Finding Meaning**: Many people who go through difficult situations find that they want to give back or contribute to society

in meaningful ways. Whether it's volunteering, mentoring, or advocating for others who have been through similar experiences, finding a **sense of purpose** can help you feel more fulfilled.

5. Surround Yourself with Positive People

The people you choose to surround yourself with can have a huge impact on your life. Seek out individuals who are supportive, who encourage you to do better, and who want to see you succeed. Avoid toxic relationships or environments that encourage bad behavior. Building a **supportive community** can help you stay motivated and focused.

6. Embrace Resilience and Patience

Rebuilding your life won't happen overnight, and it will take resilience. There will be setbacks, but it's important to **keep pushing forward**, even when things get difficult. Celebrate small victories along the way, and don't be too hard on yourself when progress is slow. **Patience with yourself** and trust in the process is crucial.

7. Find and Pursue a Higher Purpose

A key element of rebuilding a life after a criminal situation is finding a **greater purpose** or **meaning**. Some ways to explore this could include:

- **Helping Others**: Many people who have been through struggles find that working with others who are in a similar situation can be rewarding. You could consider mentoring someone who is going through what you went through.

- **Spirituality**: For some, turning to **faith or spirituality** provides a sense of purpose and hope. It offers guidance, peace, and a community that can help you stay focused on your growth.
- **Creative Outlets**: Whether it's writing, art, or music, creative expression can be incredibly therapeutic and a great way to rebuild your sense of self. It can also open up new opportunities for personal fulfillment.

8. Take Care of Your Mental and Physical Health

To truly rebuild your life, it's important to take care of your **mental** and **physical health**. Exercise, eat well, get enough sleep, and practice self-care. Good health supports mental clarity, energy, and emotional balance, all of which are essential as you rebuild your life.

Final Advice: Focus on Growth, Not Perfection

The journey to rebuilding your life is not about perfection, it's about growth. **Everyone makes mistakes**, and it's not the mistakes that define us, but how we rise from them. Focus on moving forward, learning from past experiences, and becoming the person you aspire to be. Take it one step at a time and remember that **your past does not define your future**.

There's always hope and opportunity for a better tomorrow, and with the right mindset, resources, and support, you can rebuild your life and pursue a meaningful future.

About the Author

Rick Curry
Author & Owner of Accused Federal Guide to Justice Paralegal LLC

With over 25 years of experience in federal criminal law, Rick Curry is a certified paralegal and a passionate advocate for freedom, justice, and equality. As a former federally convicted felon who has turned his life around, Rick offers a unique and powerful perspective to those facing challenges within the federal system.

Through his company, he provides legal guidance and support to individuals navigating the complexities of indictments, sentencing, appeals, and post-conviction relief.

Rick is also a published author and creative storyteller. His works include:

- *The Accused Federal Guide to Justice Handbook: A Survival Guide for Those Facing Federal Charges by the Feds, DEA, or ATF*

- *The Accused Federal Guide to Justice Handbook: A Survival Guide for Those Facing ICE & Immigration Proceedings*

- *Mirror to the Hidden Land of Buganda* (Family Fiction Series)

- *Implied Malice* (Urban Novel)
- *Malice Afterthought* (Urban Novel Part 2)

His writing bridges the gaps between law, advocacy, storytelling, educating, entertaining, and inspiring change.

The author appreciates all his readers and supporters.

Contact Information

Mailing Address:
P.O. Box 260
Rex, GA 30273-9998

Phone: (770) 334-5180

Email: accusedme23@gmail.com

Editorial assistance provided by Cheryl Adams Odeleye.

Accused Federal Guide to Justice
Paralegal Services LLC
P.O. Box 260
Rex, GA 30273
accusedme23@gmail.com

The Accused Federal Guide to Justice Handbook: A Survival Guide for Those Facing Federal Charges by the Feds, DEA, or ATF

Rick Curry, Author

This material is provided for **educational and informational purposes only**. It is not intended to serve as legal advice. Readers are encouraged to consult with a qualified legal professional for any legal matters related to their case or circumstances.

Certain references or excerpts may fall under the **"Fair Use"** doctrine of U.S. Copyright Law (17 U.S.C. § 107), which allows limited use of copyrighted material for purposes such as criticism, comment, news reporting, teaching, scholarship, or research. Any such usage within this work is intended for non-commercial, educational purposes and is in compliance with Fair Use standards.

Made in United States
Orlando, FL
04 November 2026

90200632R00174